WINDOWS ON THE WHITE HOUSE

WINDOWS ON THE WHITE HOUSE
THE STORY OF PRESIDENTIAL LIBRARIES

by Curt Smith

Diamond Communications, Inc.
South Bend, Indiana
1997

WINDOWS ON THE WHITE HOUSE
The Story of Presidential Libraries
Copyright © 1997 by Curt Smith

10 9 8 7 6 5 4 3 2 1

Manufactured in the United States of America

Diamond Communications, Inc.
Post Office Box 88
South Bend, Indiana 46624-0088
Editorial: (219) 299-9278
Orders Only: 1-800-480-3717
Fax: (219) 299-9296

Library of Congress Cataloging-in-Publication Data

Smith, Curt.
    Windows on the White House : the story of presidential libraries /
by Curt Smith.
        p.   cm.
    Includes bibliographical references (p.   ) and index.
    ISBN 1-888698-10-1
    1. Presidential libraries--United States--History.
    2. Presidential libraries--United States--Guidebooks.   I. Title.
CD3029.82.S55   1997
026'.9739--dc21
                                                            97-2584
                                                              CIP

To the America
that is Mayberry

Other Books by CURT SMITH

America's Dizzy Dean

Long Time Gone

Voices of The Game

A Fine Sense of the Ridiculous

The Storytellers

CONTENTS

"The past is never dead.
It's not even past."

— William Faulkner,
   Intruder in the Dust

ACKNOWLEDGMENTS

In William Manchester's book, *The Glory and the Dream*, Dwight Eisenhower is watching the 1952 Republican Convention on television. Would Ike be nominated for president? To ensure luck, he rubbed two charms: one, a Salvation Army coin — the other, a Boy Scout token.

To George Bush, the event mixed man and symbol. "Dwight Eisenhower," he said, "showed how 'faith, love of freedom, and energy' could change a land." The token bespoke what "presidents should recall nightly on their knees. 'Be prepared'" — the Boy Scout motto.

Many people helped prepare this book. They were generous with their time and memory. I hope *Windows on the White House* is generous toward them.

Presidents Nixon, Ford, and Bush were kind to suggest which of their contemporaries *should* have been president — and, therefore, their libraries in these pages. I also wish to thank the members of an exclusive club — past and current directors of the presidential libraries and museums — for their thought and aid.

They are, alphabetically: David Alsobrook, Roger Bridges, William Cunliffe, George Curtis, Bradley Gerratt, Larry Hackman, Daniel D. Holt, Mark Hunt, James R. Kratsas, Frank H. Mackaman, Harry J. Middleton, Verne W. Newton, Dr. Donald B. Schewe, Richard Norton Smith, John Taylor, and Dr. Timothy Walch. I am pleased that a portion of this book's proceeds will benefit the various presidential libraries' Gift Funds.

Another roll of people supplied research and/or advice. They include: Pat Anderson, Lynn Bassanese, Steve Branch, Patricia Burchfield, Kevin Cartwright, Jim Cicconi, Jim Detlefsen, Mary Finch, Allen Fisher, Gil Gonzales, Allan Goodrich, Hugh Hewitt, Shirley Joiner, Nancy Mirshah, Susan Naulty, Oonagh Paulson, Linda Casey Poepsel, Mark Renovitch, Frank Rigg, Liz Safly, Robert Schoen, E. Philip Scott, Linda Smith, Wendy Sparks, David Stanhope, Kathleen Struss, Pauline Testerman, Jim Wagner, Gary Yarrington, Richard Jacobs, former acting assistant archivist for Presidential Libraries, and Don Wilson, executive director of the Bush Library Center. All nursed this book to birth from conception.

I want to thank Jill Langford and Sharon Hill of Diamond Communications, who edited this manuscript. Juanita Dix produced the layout and design. Doug Gamble suggested the book title. Kerri Donaleski compiled the index. My wife, Sarah, and literary agent, Bobbe Siegel, showed why they are women of uncommon cloth. Finally, kudos to the presidents in this book for giving me so much to write about. Hail to the Chiefs — and their libraries, too.

PRESIDENTIAL LIBRARIES

(Listed in order of official opening)

1.   Rutherford B. Hayes Presidential Center. Fremont, Ohio.

2.   Franklin D. Roosevelt Library. Hyde Park, New York.

3.   Harry S. Truman Library. Independence, Missouri.

2003 ✓4.   Dwight D. Eisenhower Library. Abilene, Kansas.

5.   Herbert Hoover Library-Museum. West Branch, Iowa.

10-17-99 ✓6.   Lyndon Baines Johnson Library and Museum. The University of Texas campus. Austin, Texas.

✓7.   John Fitzgerald Kennedy Library. Boston, Massachusetts.

8.   Gerald R. Ford Library. The University of Michigan campus. Ann Arbor, Michigan. (The Ford Museum is in Grand Rapids, Michigan)

✓9.   Jimmy Carter Library. Atlanta, Georgia.

2001 ✓10.   Richard Nixon Library and Birthplace. Yorba Linda, California. (The National Archives in College Park, Maryland, house the Nixon papers.)

✓11.   Ronald Reagan Library and Museum. Simi Valley, California.

10-16-99 12.   George Bush Library and Museum. The Texas A&M University campus. College Station, Texas.

PROLOGUE

"PRESIDENTS, LIKE GREAT French restaurants," said Dougglas Cater, "have an ambiance all their own." Like Rashomon, their image depends on stripe and place. Was Harry Truman's a Fair, or Raw, Deal? Which brush draws Richard Nixon — Watergate President, or architect of peace? What say ye of the 1980s? A new Gilded Age, or America's millennium in the morn?

Each year, an estimated 1.5 million people visit the 12 presidential libraries. Their lure: oral history passed from one generation to another. Visit West Branch or Hyde Park or Austin or Abilene. Elitist, redolent of Thornton Wilder, or pitchfork-populist — they recall men who sought to do right, and thus achieve good.

Windows on the White House explores libraries from Hayes via Truman through Carter to Bush. Think of them as friends around a dinner table — giants, mediocrities, and/or household words. Retrieving the past, their sites retrace defeat and even tragedy — also triumph, statecraft, and an almost Tinker Bell kind of faith.

The presidency is a peculiarly American institution. This book etches how if something grabs you early — to many, what Theodore Roosevelt called the "Bully Pulpit," or John F. Kennedy "the vital center of action" — it almost never lets you go.

CHAPTER 1

STIRRINGS

EACH DECADE AIRS SYMBOLS of a special time and feel. Say 1940, and you think Kate Smith. "This is America!" said Franklin Roosevelt upon presenting her to George VI. Fast-forward to the 1970s Cocker, Cosell, and Crosby, Stills, and Nash. The 1990s blaze Madonna, Jay Leno, and Roseanne. Some term this progress.

Other names cross decades. George Burns bonded vaudeville and the VCR. Johnny Carson banished age with hale, light commentary. Bob Hope wrote continuity on the transient pulp of life. "If he didn't exist," a writer said, "you'd have to invent him as Unifier of the Generations."

Familiar, presidents stroke the tender ear of memory. Aptly, their libraries bridge, not cleave, the years. They paint more or less a blend, among other things, of duty, propriety, old-fashioned heroism, and individualism spiked by compassion and plain-speaking. Each dons hats worn in the Oval Office. Politician.

Policy-maker. Commander in Chief. Captain/chaplain.

In his landmark book, *Presidential Power*, the political scientist Richard E. Neustadt concluded that the public's picture of a chief executive "takes shape for most constituents no later than the time they first perceive him as being President (a different thing than seeing him as a candidate)." Libraries complete the photo — developing whether, say, Herbert Hoover is deemed satanic or the dream to save the land.

George Bush has said, "Americans have built presidential libraries both to document and disseminate their history." It was not always so. Preservation was once hit or miss — especially in the 19th Century. Leaving office, George Washington considered his papers private property. He took them, and led 17 successors to do the same. Each plucked files from public view. Many were later lost, purged, stolen, or ignored.

Some of Andrew Jackson's papers

vanished when the Hermitage caught fire in 1934. The heirs of Martin Van Buren destroyed part of his, as did Franklin Pierce, Ulysses Grant, and Millard Fillmore's. In 1865, Richmond burned — and most of John Tyler's papers. Federal troops carted off Zachary Taylor's. Washington's reemerged when a relative sold them to the State Department for $55,000. Lincoln's papers weren't available for public use before 1948. Until the '50s, John Quincy Adams' were locked in the Massachusetts Historical Society.

RECALL WILLIAM BENDIX IN TV'S "The Life of Riley": "What a revoltin' development this is!" Enter a pioneer anomaly — and unlikely pioneer. On May 30, 1916, the Rutherford B. Hayes Presidential Center opened to the public. Its museum and archives were unique for the next generation. Later presidents destroyed papers — or gave them haphazardly to local libraries, historical societies, and private collections.

Then, in 1937, a history student wrote a letter to Hayes' son. "I think it is particularly fitting," said Franklin Roosevelt, "that this collection [at the Hayes Center] should include, besides President Hayes' own library, his correspondence and other papers associated with his public life." A year later, he donated personal and presidential papers to the federal government — and pledged part of his estate at Hyde Park to a library and museum.

In 1939, FDR laid a cornerstone, and friends formed a nonprofit corporation to raise funds. Thus began the first presidential library under National Archives' care. A French writer was once asked what he would take if his house were on fire and he could remove one thing. "I would take the fire," he replied. Roosevelt liked what worked — the Hayes Center, as precedent and model. His papers would not be tossed like leaves to the wind!

FDR's began the cycle of presidential libraries. In 1955, Congress passed legislation — the Presidential Libraries Act — letting other presidents donate historical materials to the government with guaranty that papers would be preserved and made available. Presidents Hoover through Bush expanded the idea of Hayes and Roosevelt into a system of presidential libraries.

Some sites prefer the singular name — to wit, the Jimmy Carter Library. Others add "museum" to their formal title — e.g. the Ronald Reagan Library and Museum. This book views "library" as an umbrella — embracing both archives and museum. Today, 12 form a loose confederation.

Rutherford B. Hayes Center. Presidency: 1877-81. Opened: May 30,

1916. Location: Fremont, Ohio. Includes: more than one million pages of documents from the Hayes presidency — and 10,000 museum objects like a White House carriage. The center contains the residence and tombs of Rutherford and Lucy Hayes.

Herbert Hoover Library-Museum. Presidency: 1929-33. Opened: August 10, 1962. Location: West Branch, Iowa. Includes: records from Hoover's career in public service, rare books, a collection of valuable Chinese porcelain, and map of the 57 Nations where the Great Humanitarian fed starving peoples. His birthplace and grave — like wife Lou's — grace the 187-acre grounds.

Franklin D. Roosevelt Library. Presidency: 1933-45. Opened: June 30, 1941. Location: Hyde Park, New York. Includes: a large collection of documents, FDR's 1936 Ford Phaeton equipped with special hand controls, a small naval museum, and family mementos of the patriot, two-term governor of New York, and four-term president.

Harry S. Truman Library. Presidency: 1945-53. Opened: July 6, 1957. Location: Independence, Missouri. Includes: a replica of the Oval Office, office used by Truman in retirement, and numerous paintings by his favorite artist, Thomas Hart Benton. The 33rd president and Bess Truman are buried here.

Dwight D. Eisenhower Library. Presidency: 1953-61. Opened: May 1, 1962. Location: Abilene, Kansas. Includes: memorabilia from Ike's military days and White House years. A complex of buildings houses Ike's presidential papers and a nondenominational church. Eisenhower and his wife, Mamie, are buried here.

John Fitzgerald Kennedy Library. Presidency: 1961-63. Opened: October 20, 1979. Location: Boston, Massachusetts. Includes: a museum housed in a waterfront building designed by I.M. Pei. An exhibit features JFK's desk and rocking chair. Others invoke moments from his presidency — including the Cuban Missile Crisis, Nuclear Test Ban Treaty, and November 22, 1963.

Lyndon Baines Johnson Library and Museum. Presidency: 1963-69. Opened: May 22, 1971. Location: University of Texas at Austin, Texas. Includes: political memorabilia, an oral history project, Viet Nam War exhibit, replica of the Oval Office, conferences and symposia, and archives with 35 million pages of documents.

Richard Nixon Library and Birthplace. Presidency: 1969-74. Opened: July 19, 1990. Location: Yorba Linda, California. Includes: a replica of the Lincoln Sitting Room, White House tapes from the Watergate scandal, and Nixon's vice-presidential and pre- and post-presidential papers. His grave —

also, wife Pat's — and birthplace lie next to the library.

Gerald R. Ford Library. Presidency: 1974-77. Opened: April 27, 1981. Location: University of Michigan at Ann Arbor, Michigan. Includes: Ford's papers from his 27 years in Congress and 30 months as president. The Ford Presidential Museum opened on September 18, 1981, in Grand Rapids, Michigan, and features exhibits from the Nixon pardon to the 1976 presidential campaign.

Jimmy Carter Library. Presidency: 1977-81. Opened: October 1, 1986. Location: Atlanta, Georgia. Includes: Camp David accords, SALT II Treaty, replica of the Oval Office, exhibit on the Iran hostage crisis, and interactive video. Also, Carter's papers, objects from foreign leaders, handmade gifts from Americans, and a formal dinner setting from the White House.

Ronald Reagan Library and Museum. Presidency: 1981-89. Opened: November 4, 1991. Location: Simi Valley, California. Includes: videotapes, photographs, a replica of the Oval Office, a tribute to Nancy Reagan, the Voices of Freedom Gallery, and the largest collection of presidential material of any library — 50 million pages, or 23,500 feet.

George Bush Library and Museum. Presidency: 1989-93. Opened: November 6, 1997. Location: Texas A&M University at College Station, Texas. Includes: the George Bush Center and School of Public Service — and museum, classrooms, offices for the President and Mrs. Bush, replica of the Air Force One and Camp David offices, and artifacts from the Panama invasion and Gulf War triumph.

EACH LIBRARY WAS BUILT BY funds from private and nonfederal sources. All but Nixon's turned papers into government property by deed of gift. Only his and Hayes' are not operated and maintained by the National Archives and Records Administration. Two decades post-Watergate, Nixon's presidential papers are still contested in court. The archives controls them at its offices in College Park, Maryland.

There and elsewhere, bodies of material are culled to illumine its highest office — then put in places accessible to the public. Some denote a presidency of booming voice — some, a hauteur toward outsiders and to itself — others, of self-doubt and extempore rhetoric. All denote a map which led from Verdun to V-E Day through Viet Nam to the Persian Gulf. Libraries recall its driving — and miles covered to and from.

Their posts can become feel-good shrines: recall Bing Crosby's "Accentuate the positive." Each touts the house begun in 1792, finished in 1800, and renovated from Jacqueline Kennedy to Hillary Clinton. All serve scholars, lure laymen who regard libraries more as flesh and blood, and love/hate the city of Georgetown and Embassy Row and Lafayette Park. "They are popular places for Americans of every age," said Don Wilson, former archivist of the United States and now executive director of the Bush Library Center, "to explore a history not always learned in school."

History taught Churchill that "We shape our buildings. Thereafter, they shape us." Shaping libraries are more than 250 million pages of textual materials; five million photographs; 13.5 million feet of motion picture film; 68,000 hours of disc, audiotape, and videotape records; and 280,000 museum objects. In turn, libraries shape perception through a pastiche of eye and ear. *Exempli gratia*:

Size: Johnson's library occupies a giant 96,981 square feet. "LBJ liked being the biggest," said former press secretary George Christian. "He never wanted to be second in anything." In 1986, exempting then-President Reagan, Congress asked that future libraries be no larger than 70,000 feet.

Silhouette: Kennedy's library soars. Ford's is utilitarian; Carter's, messianic; Bush's, unpretentious. Hayes' flaunts Billy Sunday by way of Grant Wood ;

Nixon's, roots that are almost rhapsodically square.

Outlook: Truman's biographical film accents the '48 Election over Douglas MacArthur's firing. Reagan's treats Lebanon as footnote — Ike's, Little Rock as asterisk — FDR's, Supreme Court "packing" less as bungle than crusade.

Outreach: Some are museums-in-progress. Hoover's aired a 1989 display, "39 Men," of the then-39 presidents with more than 300 pieces of personal memorabilia. Johnson's exhibits have linked Teddy Roosevelt, Walt Whitman, and "the age of the flapper."

"Each library is a metaphor of the man — and like him, made up of different aspects — shape, content, architecture, message," *TIME* magazine columnist Hugh Sidey has observed. "Add it up, and it's a President's rebuttal. These guys who take the slings and arrows, who are pummeled, finally have their chance."

EDDIE GOMEZ, WHO PLAYED BASS with pianist Billy Evans, called the great jazzman's goal to "make music that balanced passion and intellect." Think of presidents as playing bass. Some speak, and you hear them squeak. Others reveal their soul.

Libraries fit music to their subject's bent: Hoover's dwells on the quaint and personal; Kennedy, the royal. The presidency can shrink a man. Libraries mix self-drama, fact, and hospitality to make him larger than he was.

Dedicating his library, Franklin Roosevelt made visitors at Hyde Park feel like a guest. Then, he tried to place it in America's psychic attic of imagery.

"It seems to me," he ad-libbed, "that the dedication of a library is in itself an act of faith. To bring together the records of the past and to house them in buildings where they will be preserved for the use of men and women in the future, a nation must believe in three things.

"It must believe in the past. It must believe in the future. It must, above all, believe in the capacity of its own people to learn from the past so that they can gain in judgment in creating their own future."

Like his America, Roosevelt believed. Today, presidential libraries await history's judgment, elusive and ephemeral. *Windows on the White House* tells how archives would no more ignore it than try to reverse the sands of time.

Where this book's presidents lived. "The White House has been pulled apart, rearranged … reassembled," wrote William Seale. "Yet it is always the same. Its idea has become its essence." *(Bush Library)*

CHAPTER 2

COLOR MY WORLD

JOHN F. KENNEDY SAID OF the presidency, "I have a nice home, the office is close by" — 50 yards from his residence — "and the pay is good." George Bush told a speech meeting, "I'm not Ronald Reagan. I couldn't be if I wanted to."

Like life, politics is chockablock with slant. Your favorite president may seem like Harold Stassen to me. Libraries reflect that gulf — recalling leaders who, depending on your point of view, were heavenly, horrific, funny, risque, humane, and/or more often human.

Few visitors to, say, Fremont or Independence are truly neutral. Most try to be fair. The artwork that follows shows the libraries of Rutherford B. Hayes, Herbert Hoover, Franklin D. Roosevelt, and Harry Truman. It etches a time less of black and white — even when the photos were — than muted tints and bold pastels: a panoply of color.

Rutherford B. Hayes Presidential Center. Fremont, Ohio. *(Hayes Center)*

Herbert Hoover Library-Museum. West Branch, Iowa. *(Hoover Library-Museum)*

Franklin D. Roosevelt Library. Hyde Park, New York. *(Roosevelt Library)*

Harry S. Truman Library. Independence, Missouri. *(Truman Library)*

CHAPTER 3

MR. CLEAN/"RUTHERFRAUD" RUTHERFORD B. HAYES CENTER

(Hayes Presidential Center)

AT ONE TIME OR ANOTHER, many presidents are deemed accidental.

Remember the military man who entered politics after the Civil War.

Rutherford Brichard Hayes formed part of the Oval Office's Long Gray Line of 1865-1901 suzerainty. Thomas Wolfe called presidents between Lincoln and TR, "The Lost Americans: their gravely vacant and bewildered faces mixed, melt, swam together. Which had the whiskers, which the burnsides, which was which?" Like madams in the dark, it was difficult to tell.

Hayes was the president who a) was 5 feet, 8 inches tall; b) had a wife named "Lemonade Lucy," who banned alcohol from the White House; c) ingrained five children with courtesy and rectitude; d) seemed sober, Victorian, a non-glamor boy; or e) embraced mellowspeak as America began to hammerlock the world. Choose any — actually, all — of the above.

This Hayes Center display re-creates the aftermath of the Battle of South Mountain, Maryland, September 14, 1862, in which Hayes, then a colonel, was wounded in the arm. *(Hayes Center)*

Hayes was a Civil War colonel and brigadier general of Ohio's 23rd at South Mountain — later, two-term Ohio congressman and three-term governor. Honor clung to him like moss to Mississippi. By 1876, the scandal of fellow GOPer Ulysses S. Grant made such men seem rare. By contrast, think of Hayes! What probity! "He serves his party best who serves his country best."

The irony is that, vowing to cleanse Washington, Hayes won the presidency in a way that briefly took his bleach and poured it down the drain.

TWO YEARS EARLIER, THE DEMO-crats had won the House of Representatives for the first time since 1858. Was honesty in the White House MIA? They now revealed their SOS for president: candidate Samuel J. Tilden, governor of New York.

Like Tilden's, change shadowed Hayes' campaign. In a century, America had turned from wilderness to settlement — agrarian to manufacturing — states rights to United States. Its states had leapt from 13 to 38 — population, 2.5 million to 46 million — area, 889,000 square miles to three million. Limits were, well, so un-American. "People here are far less raw and provincial than their fathers," said *The Nation* of America at age 100. "They have seen more ... read more ... mixed more with people or other nationalities, they have thought more and had to think more, they have spent more for ideas and given more away."

By 1876, almost one-fifth of America was foreign-born. Cities exploded in the post-war industrial boom — Philadelphia's population to nearly 750,000; New York's, a million-plus. The slickers' influx buoyed Tilden. Yet most people were rural, which favored Hayes. Eric Goldman's "MetroAmerican" belonged to a later, more urban age. Nearly 80 percent of America still lived on farms or in towns that relied on agriculture.

One hundred and eighty-five electoral votes made you president. By the morning after Election Day, Tilden had 184; Hayes, 166. Each claimed the 19 electoral votes of the only southern states still run by Republican machines built during Reconstruction. In South Carolina, Florida, and Louisiana, the GOP bought votes, controlled state offices, and junked Democratic ballots. Speakers railed, "Tilden or Blood!" Militia readied in Democratic-ruled states. Talk rose of a march on Washington. Tangible causes implied a constitutional crisis.

One paper mourned, "Did we fight a

Spiegel Grove (above) includes the Hayes residence and library and museum in the background. In the foreground: a part of the Harrison Military Trail. The main entrance (left) boasts one of the estate's six iron gates which guarded an 1877-81 entrance to the White House grounds. *(Hayes Center)*

Rutherford B. Hayes, formally attired in this pose. *(Hayes Presidential Center)*

days before Inauguration Day, Grant was packing, there was still no decision, and would-be violence whiffed the air.

That morning, Hayes' train left Columbus, Ohio, for Washington. The next day, he learned that Congress had upheld his election: Through the window, relief crested in the rain. The "Compromise of 1877" made Hayes president. It also spawned cries of "The Fraudulency" — a.k.a. "Rutherfraud B. Hayes." The commission gave Hayes the disputed states and the presidency in exchange for — what? Cynics must be credited with 20/20 sight.

Hayes withdrew the last federal troops from Dixie, named a southerner to his cabinet, gave southern control of federal patronage to Democrats, and used federal aid to help build railroads and public works. The compromise irked Democrats and regular Republicans. The former hated the result — Hayes' election — the latter, its ransom. Hayes didn't care. He intended to govern as president of all the people.

Hayes' blurring of friends and enemies frosted the GOP Old Guard. Put another way, it soon thought him an ingrate — forgetting who elected him, and why.

Civil War to make way for this?" The answer was self-evident. So the Democratic House and Republican Senate chose a 15-man commission — seven Republicans, seven Democrats, and one independent picked by Congress and the Supreme Court. The first independent was disqualified. His replacement voted Republican. Yet on March 1, 1877, two

JOHN CONNALLY ONCE SAID OF the Viet Nam /civil rights/Richard Nixon/sexual revolution early-1970s,

"Everything about it was big!" The 1870s America bequeathed to and shaped by Hayes was, as well.

The Sioux War ended with the defeat of Sitting Bull and Crazy Horse. Custer and about 265 men were killed at Little Big Horn, Montana. A land boom hit the Dakotas. Timber rights opened on public domain to settlers. The Desert Land Act brought irrigation to arid areas. Alaska celebrated its first major gold strike. George(s) Westinghouse and Eastman built empires based on genera-

tors and film, respectively. Edison patented the phonograph and invented the first practical incandescent bulb.

From 1865 to 1901, total national income quadrupled. The rural and small-town Hayes seemed a bizarre simile of an age where extravagance was king. Private and fastidious, he blared a Fred MacMurray-type of affability. "Each evening the [Hayes] family gathered in the Red Room to sing sentimental ballads," wrote Margaret B. Klapthor. "A few hymns and family prayers followed,

The formal dining room, with fireplace, at Spiegel Grove. Shunning liquor, the Hayes and their five children enjoyed traditional American food of the mid-to late-19th Century. *(Hayes Center)*

★ ★ Mr. Clean/"Rutherfraud" ★ ★

Rutherford and Lucy Hayes, shortly after their marriage (from a daguerreotype). As America's First Couple, they restored dignity and morality to the White House. (*Hayes Center*)

then the children were sent upstairs to study while the president and his wife received guests." Non-glitzy, he non-spellbound on the stump. *The New York Times* caught the upside of Hayes' few appearances in the '76 campaign: "[He is] not going to talk himself out of the Presidency." The down was that he might make the presidency seem somehow punier than it was.

It never happened. Hayes restored the presidency's moral rubric. Of and from America's polite respectability, he also surprised by treating power as arcadia, not ball and chain. Hayes signed a treaty with China giving America the right to regulate "coolie" immigration — but vetoed a Chinese exclusion bill because it mocked the 1868 Burlingame Treaty with China. He let the Army pursue bandits into Mexico, made cabinet selections without senatorial advice, and

Spiegel Grove's large drawing room, with a piano and other artifacts of the Gilded Age. Said center director Roger Bridges: "It is a residence full of antiques." *(Hayes Center)*

renewed presidential fiat by vetoing repeal of federal regulation of some elections in the South.

Twelve of Hayes' 13 vetoes were upheld. The exception was the Bland-Allison Bill pledging the government to purchase, at market price, two to four millions dollars worth of silver each month to spur production of the metal. By 1889, he said, "If a Napoleon ever became President, he could make the executive almost what he wished to make it." What Hayes wished was for

business to occupy a sustaining niche.

Its umbilical cord was railroads. By 1880, the U.S. brandished 93,262 miles of line. Workers rebelled at profit-hoarding, and rioted in Baltimore, St. Louis, Pittsburgh, Chicago, and San Francisco. "It is wrong to call this a strike," a newspaper said. "It is a labor revolution." It was neither — only workers slowly stirring, like a still stream shedding ice.

In 1877, Hayes called out the Army on petition of governors of West Virginia, Maryland, Pennsylvania, and Illinois to end the strike. The precedent made government a first-time diner at arbitration's table. More lasting was the lesson, and danger, of trying to sever politics from policy.

Hayes thought the other party capable of episodic good will. He temporized as his own party was veering right, and was left in the middle. The result — a Flying Dutchman, *sans* political port, who rued the saw, "Dance with the one who brung you." Before long Hayes felt like a wallflower at the ball.

A POLITICAL SAW ORDAINS, "IF you want a friend in Washington, get a dog." Supposed friends — state bosses like Don Cameron in Pennsylvania, Zachariah Chandler in Michigan, New York's Roscoe Conkling, and Maine's James Blaine — had helped put Hayes in the White House. They now came to feel that he treated them like a Rottweiler.

Freeze-frame the late 1870s. Bosses controlled appointments from cabinet head to train conductor. Hayes attacked their patronage, and cloaked federal jobs

The Hayes' master bedroom features a period fireplace and canopy bed. This, and the residence's other rooms, are furnished in the ornate style of the Victorian era. *(Hayes Center)*

The Hayes Museum and Library, a structure of classic architecture built of gray Ohio sandstone, contains one floor of presidential archives and two floors of exhibits. *(Hayes Center)*

in civil service. In June 1877, he issued an executive order banning federal appointees from politicking — later, asking a Conkling appointee, Chester A. Arthur, to resign as Collector of the Port of New York.

Arthur and another custom official were fired for plotting with importers and officials to cheat the government. Mate: Conkling blocked confirmation of Hayes' replacements for the sacked officials. Checkmate: In 1878, Hayes elected them with Democratic help. Later, Hayes wrote in his diary: "My sole right to make appointments is tacitly conceded." Not conceded was a split Repub-

lican Party or an 1880 convention which regarded him as a leper at a bazaar.

By then, the 19th president had spurned renomination. He had little choice. Thomas Nast, longtime chief political cartoonist for *Harper's Weekly*, drew a cartoon of a Democratic tiger wearing a sign, "For Republican Lamb, inquire within." Better president than politician, Hayes' waves of loyalty waned. Leaving office, America respected him. The GOP detested him. Exquisitely second-guessable, he strengthened the office and redeemed the presidency after Grant.

Today, many successors — Garfield,

★ ★ Mr. Clean/"Rutherfraud" ★ ★

McKinley, even Arthur — match Hayes in identity. Perhaps the reason is a reverse twist of phrase. It is said that nothing so distinguishes someone's life as his leaving it. Nothing so distinguished Rutherford B. Hayes' administration as his achieving it.

Rutherford B. Hayes Center, Spiegel Grove, Fremont, Ohio 43420-2796. Roger Bridges, Director. Phone: (419) 332-2081. Fax:(419) 332-4952. Web site: http://www.rbhayes.org.

Visitors have included: President Harding; Senators John Glenn and Mark Hatfield; Secretary of War Newton Baker; Secretary of State Robert Lansing; Secretary of the Navy Chester Nimitz; four governors of Ohio, including James Rhodes.

Hours: Museum and house—Monday through Saturday, 9 A.M. to 5 P.M. Sunday and holidays, noon to 5 P.M. Library—Monday through Saturday, 9 A.M. to 5 P.M. Open every day, except New Year's Day, Thanksgiving, and Christmas. Admission: Library, free. Museum or house: Children age 5 years and under, free. Age 6 through 12, $1. Age 13 through 60, $4. Seniors over 60, $3.25. Free parking. Library gift shop is open during regular hours.

THE LATE CRITIC WILLIAM A. Henry III wrote of America's "purple mountain majesties, amber waves of grain, small-town school marms, the cavalry to the rescue, Norman Rockwell Thanksgivings, the flag-raising at Iwo Jima, the World Series, and astronauts landing on the moon." All seemed "interlocked because they, in turn, have evoked a swelling sense of personal participation in national [too, personal] pride and purpose."

Main Street's bandstand of nostalgia, faith, and myth hosts the only presidential library and museum — save Richard Nixon's — not operated by the National Archives. The Rutherford B. Hayes Center relies on private funding, is tied to the Ohio Historical Society, and hails a life — and age. Unlike Nixon's, it houses original papers from Hayes' presidency. Like, say, Harry Truman's, the structure woos, but does not overwhelm, a visitor.

To find Fremont, Ohio, drive north from Washington, D.C., then west at the Breezewood exit on the Pennsylvania Turnpike. The road to Pittsburgh mixes hills heavy with farmland and towns shot by Ansel Adams. Entering Ohio, you pass woods, barns, and dark-gold fields. The only library devoted to a 19th-Century — and America's 19th — president

An elk horn chair, given Hayes by California hunter and trapper Seth Kinman in 1876. It is on exhibit in the museum. *(Hayes Center)*

dots its northwest corridor. Welcome Hayes as brick and mortar — and a history as sturdy as a wooden post.

About 140 years ago, Hayes' bachelor uncle and legal guardian began buying land in Lower Sandusky, as Fremont was then called. One day, the local businessman came upon a lush drop-dead tract. Its forest stand recalled German fairy tales of his youth. Sardis Birchard especially liked the clear pools of water after rain that evoked the German word *spiegel*: mirror. He built a house, named the 25-acre estate "Spiegel Grove," and gave it to his nephew.

In 1873, Hayes made the triangular plot his permanent home between second and third terms as governor of Ohio. "Hayes fell in love with it," said Hayes

Center director Roger Bridges, "and started adding to the house as governor. When he left as president [1881], he came back for good."

Ultimately, three generations of Hayes lived there before the home opened to the public. In 1910, the family deeded its estate to the State of Ohio, as a private residence, privately supported and maintained, for Hayes' heirs. It was to be "occupied or used [only] ... for residential purposes ... to the end of preserving it in its original condition as a typical home of the last half of the Nineteenth Century."

On May 30, 1916, a next-door building was dedicated for the first presidential archives and museum. The home was now part of a center — and unique for the next 25 years.

"TRY TO FRAME THE MOMENT," said Bridges. "It wouldn't happen again till Franklin Roosevelt [1941], and it hadn't occurred before — a presidential library opening. A war had begun, and America sensed it might enter. The whole event was bi-partisan, small town on parade."

Newton Baker, secretary of war, represented President Wilson. Groups linked to Hayes sent envoys to the exercises — the 23rd Ohio Regiment Association; Eugene Rawson Post, G.A.R.; Sandusky County Bar Association;

Grand Army of the Republic; and Military Order of the Loyal Legion of the United States, among others.

So far, and good. The bad pertained to size. The gray Ohio sandstone site was only 15 percent as large as today's library. Hayes' son, Webb, funded an annex, completed and dedicated on October 4, 1922 — the centennial celebration of Hayes' birth. "The growth let us expand our sights," said Webb Hayes III, Hayes' great-grandson. "Today, we document the Golden Age — 1876 through the early 1900s — through one man's career. Actually, careers — lawyer, congressman, governor, Army officer, president

— in a different America, but a precursor to today. Government was smaller, but had a role then, like now."

The Hayes Library and Museum Building recalls an age, not life, near a memorial entrance to Spiegel Grove. The museum occupies the first two floors — the library, a third. Material is family materiel: President Hayes' 12,000-volume personal library, books of Lucy's and their children, letters, diaries, scrapbooks, ledgers, photo albums, and keepsakes of their personal and public lives. By way of emphasis, the library-museum also charts:

• Hayes' "attack of geneological

The Gun Room, with military weapons collected by Hayes and members of his family. In the foreground is an antique Chinese cannon captured during the Boxer Rebellion. *(Hayes Center)*

mania," as he wrote "Uncle Scott" on March 4, 1870. "It came on about ten days ago, superinduced by reading a family tree which a friend sent me. I have got up into the Cooke tree and am lost. Can you help me out?"

• Most presidential sites are national. Hayes' is also regional. Photos render post-1840 Ohio history, especially local Sandusky County. A researcher can cull the 1820-1920 Ohio census, and atlases and history books from almost every Buckeye county.

• Seventy thousand of the library's 100,000-plus volumes sketch Hayes' Golden, or Gilded, Age. Ibid, thousands of pamphlets and periodicals, a collection of maps, photographs, and pictures, and Hayes' papers.

• The library charts Hayes' interests like Great Lakes shipping, Negro history, monetary and prison reform, the American Indian, and Civil War and its reconstruction. Also: collections by William Dean Howells and Rendell Rhoades Croquet and Lyman Lincoln's on Abraham Lincoln and manuscripts of Supreme Court Justice Stanley Matthews and Senator John Sherman.

• Thomas Nast (1840-1902) was America's first great political cartoonist. The library tenders Nast's writings, photos, artifacts, and original drawings of tokens that he bore and/or drew: the Tammany Tiger, Republican elephant,

Columbia, and, aptly, Santa Claus. Glad tidings await at this Woodstock for the middle class.

A VISITOR QUICKLY DUBS SPIEGEL Grove — like Hayes — pristine, right-minded, precise, and sentimental. One exhibit offers toy "O" gauge trains, typical of the 1880s, that run under the museum Christmas tree and in a gallery winter scene. Another grows herbs and flowers similar to those of Victorian USA.

Hayes' souvenirs include his Civil War military field equipment, Mrs. Hayes' wedding dress and first lady gowns, the old family carriage, and a doll's house of the president's only daughter, Fanny. All show a man "[whose] American ancestors were sturdy pioneers," said Hayes' biographer, Charles R. Williams. "Honest, wholesome, industrious, God-fearing folk, doing faithfully their duty to family and state."

Hayes' Valhalla sees its duty as hailing keepsakes of a time. "Few libraries have the different parts that we do," said Bridges. "A museum of classic architecture with two floors of exhibits. A residence full of antiques [and red parlor, Hayes' favorite room, untouched by renovation]. An adjacent restored two-story home that hosts weddings and receptions." At the six estate entrances are iron gates which guarded an 1877-81 entrance to the White House grounds and were donated by Congress in 1928.

Outside, near the monument at the Hayes' graves, lies a final fillip — a trail dividing Spiegel Grove for half-a-mile. Three centuries ago Huron Indians were said to have built two walled towns, on opposite sides of the Sandusky River, on a trail between the Great Lakes and the Scioto and Ohio rivers. The Sandusky Scioto Indian Trail was used by early French explorers and missionaries; then, French and Indians in their war against British settlers; later, as a Revolutionary War highway and War of 1812 supply trail for William H. Harrison against the British and their Indian allies.

Today, Harrison's route of troops and supply wagons — renamed the Harrison Military Trail — evokes a Conestoga of frontier names. Daniel Boone and Simon Kenton trekked it as prisoners of the Indians. "So did Richard Johnson, vice president under James Buchanan," said Webb Hayes III, "and Indians like Red Jacket, Pontiac, and the Seneca chiefs Hard Hickory and Seneca John."

THE HARRISON TRAIL ENAMORED Hayes, who retold stories of its cock-a-hoop past. Guests heard how Indians bound captive maiden Peggy Fleming, or Mrs. Hayes' father camped under "Grandfather's Oak" during the War of 1812. Grab a cigar. Devour brandy. Hayes then took you to the tree.

The Hayes family carriage is among many museum artifacts on display to the public. In 1877-81, millions read about it — to them, the presidential limousine of its day. *(Hayes Center)*

At an 1877 reunion of his old regiment, the 23rd Ohio, Hayes began the custom of naming trees — that year's, the "Reunion Oaks" — in honor of colleagues like Philip H. Sheridan and William McKinley. Spiegel trees now bear the names of other guests like General William Tecumseh Sherman, and Presidents Garfield, Cleveland, Harding, and Taft.

Roots and leaves merge in place, and heart. "Everyone has to have a place to go back to," Hayes once said. "Spiegel Grove is that place for me."

Dedication excerpts, May 30, 1916.

"The best part of his heritage from his clean-living forebears was a sound physical constitution, a clear and active mind, a tradition of conscientious rectitude of conduct, and a scrupulous sense of duty. What better endowment could one desire for a lad, provided he have the environment and opportunity to develop his powers, and provided he have the will to make the most of himself?" — Charles R. Williams, author of Hayes' biography, *The Life of Rutherford Birchard Hayes*

"The controlling principle of his life was simplicity itself. It was under all conditions and in all circumstances, to do what he believed to be right. The motto of the ... family of Hayes from which he traced his descent, was the single Latin word Recte. *That is the adverb form of the world that means straight or right. In all his conduct, public and private, Mr. Hayes exemplified that motto. He was 'straight' in thought and action; he moved in right lines; his dealings were void of indirection or equivocation."*
— C. R. Williams

"The judgment of posterity, I believe, will pronounce Mr. Hayes' administration one of the cleanest, sanest, most efficient administrations in our history. No breath of scandal ever sullied its fair fame. In all its relations, domestic and foreign, honesty, efficiency, and sound decisions, coupled with dignity and courtesy, prevailed." — C. R. Williams

"Mr. Hayes returned gladly to Spiegel Grove, when his term as President expired, but not to a life of dignified leisure only. During the 12 years that still remained to him, he devoted all his thought and energy, freely and without reward, to the furtherance of worthy benevolent causes — to the interests of the old soldiers, to education in the South and to the universities of Ohio, to the advocacy of manual training in the public schools, [and] to the amelioration of the condition of the freedmen ... In all these fields

of effort he was a leader and not a follower." — C. R. Williams

★ ★ ★

Directions: From the North, take Interstate 75. Go east at Interstate 80/90 (Ohio Turnpike). Take Exit 6 south to Fremont. Follow signs to the Hayes Center. From the East, take I-80/90 west. Take Exit 6 south to Fremont. From the South, take I-75 north. Exit at Ohio Highway 6 and go east to Fremont. From the West, take I-80/90 east. Take Exit 6 south to Fremont.

The Hayes' residence at Spiegel Grove. Said America's 19th president in 1885: "For me, I can say without doubt that it is unlike any place on earth." *(Hayes Center)*

CHAPTER 4

QUAKER ALONE
HERBERT HOOVER LIBRARY-MUSEUM

(Underwood & Underwood)

RETURN TO A TIME OF PRE-fiber optics, downlinking, and satellite telegraphy. The cathode fun house was not a household core, and radio chatted as around a pot-bellied stove. In 1928, Charles Lindbergh endorsed Herbert Hoover for president. A song on the wireless replied with praise-by-association:

"You remember Hoover, back in the war.

"Saved us from the Kaiser, now he'll give us something more.

"He'll serve as the President of the land of the free.

"If he's good enough for Lindy, he's good enough for me."

Herbert Hoover was modest, honest, and seemed good enough for America. Self-made, he met success in education, business, travel, and government. Think of him as Fortune's Child who became its Dead-End Kid as president. Victim, or villain? Debate still swirls. His luck ran out too soon.

"[His] incomparable encomium,"

Much of what Hoover was sprang from this clean and proper site — the 1874 birthplace of America's 31st president in West Branch, Iowa, then-population, 350. *(Hoover Library-Museum)*

said writer Raymond Henle, "[was] that he saved more humans from starvation than any man who walked the earth." Yet his name was defined in Detroit, Chicago, and St. Louis shantytowns of the jobless down by rivers. "Hooverville" was as subtle as a Jack Dempsey hook.

Few found malice in a shy, gentle Quaker whose modesty and propriety, not newly formed, were neither bogus nor offensive. When he died on October 20, 1964, a memorial postage stamp conveyed the epitaph "Engineer, President, Humanitarian." It is fair to ask how many thought, "Two out of three ain't bad."

BORN IN WEST BRANCH, IOWA, and orphaned at three, Hoover was raised by various aunts and uncles. Poor from childhood, he found solace in tenacity. Work led to a new tuition-free university in 1891 founded by Senator Stanford in California. Hoover majored in geology, took odd jobs, and "practically lived in the lab," a classmate said. One reason was another would-be geologist — his future wife, Lou Henry.

Hoover flaunted a Sybil-like polarity: Self-denial was noble, but money sublime. Graduating in 1895, he pushed ore cars in Nevada, managed mines for the British firm of Bewick, Moreing, and Co., and became its China representative and junior partner. In Burma, he found silver and zinc deposits which made him a multimillionaire engineer. Hoover

Hoover helped feed millions during the War to End All Wars. He did the same after World War II. Said former President Harry Truman: "What more can a man do?" *(Underwood & Underwood)*

later stumbled over impromptu material. Now, he ad-libbed, "If a man has not made a million dollars by the time he is forty, he is not worth much."

At 36, Hoover was said to be worth at least $3 million. He formed his own business and wrote *Principles of Mining*, the standard bible for a generation of engineers. Yet thy Brother's Keeper was not something to take or leave. So he fled engineering in World War I to serve as head of the Commission for Belgian Relief and America's wartime food administra-tor — then, entered politics, was secretary of commerce in the Harding and Coolidge administrations, and spurred flood recovery in 1920s Mississippi. His persona dazzled: Everyman with a heart, strutting superb-for-any-age ability.

In 1928, Calvin Coolidge said, "I do not choose to run." Hoover, who did, be-came the Republican presidential nomi-nee. Like Majority America, he was ru-ral, Prohibition, and Protestant. The Democrats nominated the surpassing personality of the big city in the flesh —

New York Governor Alfred E. Smith — Tammany Hall, broken speech, anti-Prohibition, and Catholic. "We must protect for the world," Hoover said of civic Zion, "this Gibraltar of western civilization." Smith got 15 million votes to Hoover's 21 million, and lost New York and five states in the Solid South.

In his book, *Leadership In the Modern Presidency*, Fred I. Greenstein noted: "In Hoover's time, [he] still found it possible to carry on the leisurely nineteenth-century ... tradition of personally greeting any person who cared to join the reception line leading into the White House." Most perceived in Hoover, having done, a can-do certitude. Wall Street equaled wealth, which spurred jobs, which nurtured growth. Nothing had prepared him for a world in which logic wore not a stitch.

Prosperity garbed America on Inauguration Day 1929. In 39 months, the average of common stock prices on the New York Stock Exchange had leaped by 123 percent. Visiting New York, F. Scott Fitzgerald found that his barber had retired with $500,000 from the market. John Raskob, a director of General Motors, wrote in *Ladies Home Journal* of saving and investing in stocks, "I am firm in my belief that anyone not only can be rich but ought to be rich." Raskob was chairman of the Democratic National Committee. America-in-bloom-

forever was a view crossing party lines.

"We in America," Hoover echoed, "are nearer the final triumph over poverty than ever before in the history of any land." He ignored calamity's midwife — fear. By October 24, 1929 — Black Thursday — stock sales had soared over the past several days. Inevitably, prices fell. Most brokers wanted to sell. Investors tried to protect securities by putting up cash as collateral. On October 29, 16,410,030 shares were traded. Thousands of speculators threw their holdings into the pit.

THE OFFSHOOT WAS AN AMERICA so far lost in time and place that even Ripley disbelieved it. Bread lines dotted city blocks. So did soup kitchens, pleas for one meal a day, apples for sale ("A nickel, mister"), billboards declaring, "I will share." Men pounded pavement in search for employment. Winter nights went unmarked by heat. "Happy Days Are Here Again" denoted dirge, not melody. The age reeked of "Brother, Can You Spare a Dime?"

Churchill said of Stalin's Russia, "It is a riddle wrapped in a mystery inside an enigma." Ditto, the Great Depression — formerly, Depression — nee, recession. Bank failures spiraled. Contagion roiled the 12 or 15 or 16 million unemployed. Rusted cars served as tents ("Hoover hovels") where at night a jack rabbit (a

West Branch has changed little since Hoover first walked its streets in the 1870s. "If you want to know me," he once said in a rare twist of introspection, "go there." *(John Kofoed)*

"Hoover dog") flanked men asleep on benches. The newspaper cloaking them was a "Hoover blanket." Alone and in the dock, Hoover beseeched a jury — America — which pronounced him unfit to serve.

As president, he had subsidized air-mail, backed the Boulder and Grand Coulee dams, improved the federal prison system, reorganized the F.B.I., and reordered the federal conservation pro-gram. No matter. Most now thought him a reverse Midas. Punch-drunk, Hoover rallied to jaw-bone — be patient; the economy was "on a sound and prosper-ous basis." Be of good cheer! The worst is over! How many listened, or believed?

Whose fault was it that he seemed unmoved by pain and amnesic to-ward Depression? Hoover's? — in '60s parlance, lacking "ooh-ah." Voters? Hoover's forte was depth, not flim-flam. Luck? Shell shocked, you wanted loaves and fishes. Who can say? Only later did America see him as skin and bones, not catchphrase or caricature. The irony is that it missed a president — Herbert Hoover! — for the first time affirming

Washington's duty to protect the vulnerable against vagary.

It is true that Hoover was slow to act. In 1930, Congress asked federal taxes to sustain a federal relief fund. He refused. People would stop giving to private and community groups. For a long time Hoover vowed that charity could support the needy. Yet ultimately, he asked business to up wages; labor, ban strikes; bankers, save banks through a National Credit Association. Anything to quell nightmare's dark, mewling squall.

Essentially, Hooverism after 1930 blended federal public works, roads, and schools, and private, state, and municipal construction — reform bills in banking, securities, power company regulation, and railroad deregulation — and the Federal Reserve Board, Home Loan Bank System, and Reconstruction Finance Corporation to spur credit, save homes, and lend funds to states. "Apart from the Roosevelt measures of reform," wrote Walter Lippman, "all the major features of the Roosevelt program were anticipated by Mr. Hoover." Sadly, America judged him by 1929's "The slump is temporary. Wait for sales to rise." Many could not accept that he now wanted government as a guest.

As a child, he cast for trout in California. Post-Black Thursday, millions went fishing over Hoover. The end was anticlimax. In 1932, Franklin Roosevelt's vice-presidential nominee, John Nance Garner, said that all FDR had to do to win was live until election. Editor William Allen White backed Hoover, but saw the writing on the wall. "A fool who can lead," he said, "is better than a wise man who fumbles." Roosevelt won by more than seven million votes.

Foes-turned-friends: Two Midwesterners converse. *(Library-Museum)*

WHEN GEORGE BUSH LEFT THE White House, he read a book — *Farewell to the Chief* — "about the way past presidents have made the transition to private life." It showed Harry Truman embracing party politics — Teddy Roosevelt lashing special interests — and Hoover living a life of good works. This model impressed Bush most.

Hoover's post-presidency made honor a made-for-life daybook. He became the GOP's Grand Old Man — addressing 10 national conventions from

Hoover (first row, third from right) and his cabinet pose for a portrait. Writes the author: "Victim, or villain? Debate still swirls. His luck ran out too soon." *(Library-Museum)*

1924 through '60 — and helped found the Boys Club of America. After World War II, Hoover went to Europe to feed refugees. "The humanism of our system demands the protection of the suffering and the unfortunate," he said of duty. "It places prime responsibility upon the individual for the welfare of his neighbor."

Lauded, hated, undone, remade, Hoover outlasted more than crushed the sketchmarks of a lifetime. What a peregrination! Boyhood loneliness to wealth, power, pride, and fall through ignominy via fatalism to what Quakers term "peace at the center." What disparity! Like Bush, life to Hoover meant saving others. Yet his solicitude verified the Puritan canon of inner-directedness.

America felt he ignored her pain. One wonders if she later heard his cry. Hoover rarely spoke of 1929; it remained a long-ago, locked-up room. The miracle is that he turned inward, but not bitter, and found a last outpost of faith. Perhaps he had no choice. His faith — in God, man, and history — was not blind but timeless, and had long ago settled into his bones.

★ ★ ★

Herbert Hoover Library-Museum. Dr. Timothy Walch, Acting Director. 210 Parkside Drive, P.O. Box 488, West

Branch, Iowa 52358-0488. Phone: (319) 643-5301. Fax: (319) 643-5825. Web site: http://www.nara.gov.

Visitors have included: Presidents Truman, Eisenhower, Johnson, Nixon, Ford, and Reagan. First Ladies Mamie Eisenhower, Lady Bird Johnson, Pat Nixon, and Rosalynn Carter. Vice President Dan Quayle. Supreme Court Justice Sandra Day O'Connor. Secretary of Defense Caspar Weinberger. Senators Charles Grassley and Mark Hatfield. Recent Iowa Republican governors. Writer William F. Buckley. Historian David McCullough.

Hours: Daily, 9 A.M. to 5 P.M. Open every day, except New Year's Day, Thanksgiving, and Christmas. Admission: Children age 15 years and under and members of the Hoover Presidential Library Association, free. Age 16 to 61, $2. Seniors 62 and over, $1. Golden Eagle, Golden Age, and Golden Access passports honored. Group tours are urged to make arrangements prior to visit. Free parking. Library gift shop is open during regular hours.

MANY PRESIDENTIAL LIBRARIES have endured a long and winding road.

The Kennedy Library was to lie in Cambridge until residential protest kicked it to a shoreline site. Jimmy Carter's library overcame jibes about an access road through toni neighborhoods of Atlanta. A Reagan library at Stanford died due to student and faculty opposition. The Nixon Library was seduced, then dropped, by Duke University, the University of California at Irvine, and San Clemente, the home of RN's Western White House.

In West Branch, Iowa, people fussed that Herbert Hoover's library might erode the tax base — and a four-lane road, besoil the town. "Interestingly, the Hoover Library is now seen as the greatest asset in West Branch," recalled John

Herbert Hoover Library-Museum. West Branch, Iowa. Dedicated on August 10, 1962, it honors the admired and reviled humanitarian, engineer, and former president. *(Library-Museum)*

Hoover, in the Oval Office. Shy and stoic, he brooked contempt to rehabilitate his public image and serve America after leaving the presidency in 1933. *(Library-Museum)*

Fawcett, former National Archives assistant archivist for presidential libraries and native of the tiny (pop. 3,100) farm community. "There's been a total turnaround in how the community feels. They're even trying to revive the old four-lane road plans."

Hoover's presidency is revived in the town that peopled 350 at the time of his 1874 birth. "People come to West Branch with the image of a do-nothing, or at least ineffective, president," said Hoover Library-Museum director Timothy Walch. "Instead, they see a varied human life. Most presidential libraries celebrate the office. Ours is more human, and focuses on Hoover the hu-

manitarian, not president. We're a lot smaller in terms of square footage than most libraries. But we cover the longest life [Hoover died at 90] through all its peaks and valleys. Hoover knew — and we present them — both."

Reviled for decades, Hoover was esteemed by his death in 1964. His logic befit Lazarus: "I outlived the bastards." On August 12, 1965, the 186-acre Herbert Hoover National Historic Site was designated to preserve historically important properties. Its park links three areas that walk Hoover's road from orphan to president to outcast and elder statesman.

• The birthplace cottage (14 by 20 feet, built by Jesse Hoover and father Eli in 1871) and related historic structures (a Friends meeting house, one-room schoolhouse, and blacksmith shop operated by Hoover's father) are open to the public. They evoke 1870s West Branch. Nearby, 16 turn-of-the-century downtown buildings grace the National Register of Historic Places.

• The library-museum houses Hoover's papers and books and objects linked to his career. "Santayana rightly said, 'Those who do not remember the past are condemned to relive it,'" Hoover said on August 10, 1962, his

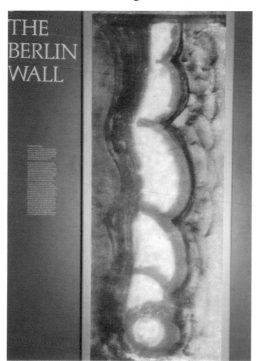

Hoover often expressed the hope that the Berlin Wall would come down. It did, a quarter-century after his death. A piece stands today in the library-museum. *(Library-Museum)*

88th birthday, at the library dedication. "These institutions are the repositories of such experience — right off the griddle. In these records there are, no doubt, unfavorable remarks made by our political opponents, as well as expressions of appreciation and affection by our friends." In West Branch, the latter trumps the field.

• A short trip leads to the gravesite near Hoover's birthplace, where he and Mrs. Hoover are buried. Close your eyes, and "think of Iowa as I saw it through the eyes of a ten-year old boy — and the eyes of all ten-year old Iowa boys ... filled with the wonders of Iowa's streams and woods, of the mystery of growing crops," Hoover said in 1962. "His days should be filled with adventure and great undertakings, with participation in good and comforting things."

THREE DECADES LATER, THE Hoover Library-Museum was rededicated — bigger and, to a layman or scholar, better — after an $8 million public and private facelift. The building includes a 180-seat auditorium and new exhibits that alternate in the William Quarton Gallery. Its seven million documentary pages lure scholars (more than 2,000 from every state and a dozen countries) and other visitors (2.7 million through 1995). Many explore seven galleries that cart them to other lands.

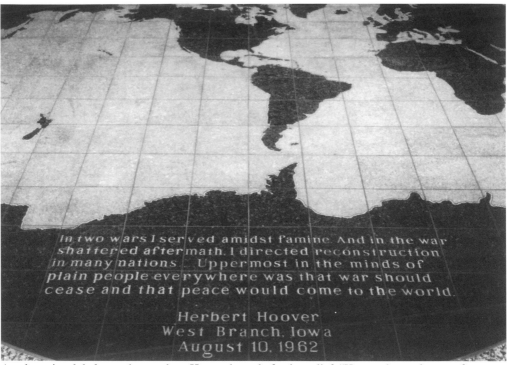

In two wars I served amidst famine. And in the war shattered aftermath, I directed reconstruction in many nations. Uppermost in the minds of plain people everywhere was that war should cease and that peace would come to the world.

Herbert Hoover
West Branch, Iowa
August 10, 1962

A red granite global map shows where Hoover brought famine relief. "He saved more humans from starvation," a writer said, "than any man who walked on earth." *(Library-Museum)*

Guests see an orientation film, then enter the rotunda: A 16-foot red granite global map uses 57 sheaves of wheat to show each country that got Hoover's disaster relief. Next, Gallery One — "Years of Adventure," linking Western Australia and a living room in Tientsin, China, during the Boxer Rebellion — and "Humanitarian Gallery." Take your choice — flower sacks sent to Hoover by American aid recipients, a likeness of a World War I Belgian food warehouse, and video theatre with buttons that brandish tales of World War I survivors.

From there, hail the Roaring '20s —

a.k.a. "Enterprise Gallery" — a montage of sights, sounds, and Hoover's deeds as secretary of commerce: fire safety codes, building material standards, and highway safety rules. Play the Hoover Quote Game, an historic electronic mix and match. Then, stand on a March 4, 1929 inaugural platform, view a multi-screen video of America BD — Before Depression — and enjoy the "President's Gallery." Films show Hoover telling what he hoped to do as president. Respond by computer-voting: How did Hoover manage 1929-33?

"To most Americans," an exhibit

reads, "the president was a remote, grim-faced man in a blue double-breasted suit. They saw none of his private anguish." Lou Hoover tried to ease it. Gallery Six re-creates the fishing cabin that she designed for her husband in the Blue Ridge Mountains. Through the windows, see her authentic home movies of the time.

Finally, review Hoover's post-presidential career in "Years of Struggle and Accomplishment." The gallery copies two rooms from Hoover's suite (31A) at New York's Waldorf Towers. A ten-strike is its period RCA television on which Hoover watched the World Series a week before his death. "Years" ends

with a lifesize diorama of Hoover's Columbia — fishing. It taught democracy, he said, for all men were created equal before fish.

THE REDESIGNED LIBRARY-MUseum has nearly twice the space of the original. Its growth spurred the Herbert Hoover Oral History Program — at present, 336 interviews — and written documentation. In addition to Hoover's papers, holdings include manuscripts of Lewis Strauss, Gerald P. Nye, Felix Morley, Clark Mollenhoff, Robert E. Wood, Westbrook Pegler, and Laura Ingalls Wilder. More than 140

Hoover lived his final years in Suite 31A of New York's elegant Waldorf Towers. Shown is the living room precisely re-created in the West Branch museum. *(Library-Museum)*

collections make the library a center for the study of farm economics, famine relief, atomic energy, conservative journalism, and government reorganization.

"Each of the presidential libraries has its own unique history, and identity," said Walch. Hoover's has evolved from exhibits on World War I (complete with walk-through trench), a bravura display of presidential gifts, and the odd fondness between Hoover and Harry Truman. "Yours has been a friendship that has reached deeper into my life than you know," Hoover wrote him in 1962. Added Walch: "Respect replaced enmity for poor farmboys who struggled upward and lived in the shadow of FDR." Other

recent or planned temporary displays include the Civil War, history of television, and the library's most popular-ever exhibit — "39 Men" — which crowned the winter of 1988-89.

"39 Men" linked artifacts from America's then-39 presidents. See John F. Kennedy's rocking chair and Calvin Coolidge's electric horse. Dwight Eisenhower's golf clubs, a piece of Grover Cleveland's wedding cake, and a signed copy of Lincoln's Emancipation Proclamation. Another temporary exhibit — "Dining at the White House" — showed Hoover as, uh, not exactly a gourmet.

"I'm not using my body," he ex-

Lou and Herbert Hoover began collecting K'ang and Ming porcelains during their time in China. Museum guests see an extensive collection on display. *(Library-Museum)*

plained. "An engineer does not stroke the engine unless there is a considerable amount of power to be exerted." During the Depression, Quaker etiquette yielded to Quaker efficiency. Hoover gobbled meals to get back to work — devouring five courses in 11 minutes.

"VISITORS COME TO WEST Branch," laughed Walch, "and see recipes and Depression, but also the co-founder of CARE and UNICEF. They view the texture of a life, which is how Mr. Hoover would have wanted it. He liked to be judged on deeds, not rhetoric. Take his speeches. He was one of the last presidents to write his own, and they reflect his engineering background. They are deadly dull, laden with statistics, yet they're the real Hoover. We show a man in more than two dimensions, amid the times in which he lived."

You relive them each August at the birthday celebration, "Hooverfest." They thrive on Downey Street in West Branch, in period houses near the Cottage, and on the Isaac Miles Farm — its land restored like the tall-grass prairie Hoover inhaled as a boy. Traipse to church, visit a harness shop, or hear a concert at the bandstand across Parkside Drive on the village green. Suddenly, it's 1874.

"Our people are deeply troubled, not only about the turbulent world around us but also with internal problems which haunt our days and nights," Hoover said in 1962. "There are many despairing voices. There are many undertones of discouragement. The press headlines imply that corruption, crime, divorce, youthful delinquency, and Hollywood love trysts are our national occupation. And amid all these voices there is a cry that the American way of life is on its way to decline and fall. I do not believe it."

Few do, visiting West Branch.

Dedication excerpts, August 10, 1962.

"I think the world of him [Hoover]. He did a job for me that nobody else in the world could have done. He kept millions of people from starving to death after the Second World War just as he did after the First World War for Woodrow Wilson, and when I asked him if he would be willing to do the job he never hesitated one minute. He said, 'Yes, Mr. President. I'll do it.' And he did a most wonderful job of keeping these people from starving, and what more can a man do?" — Harry Truman

"As a boy of ten, I was taken from this village to the Far West 78 years ago. My only material assets were two dimes in my pocket, the suit of clothes I wore. I had some extra underpinnings provided

by loving aunts. But I carried from here something more precious ... I carried with me the family disciplines of hard work. That included picking potato bugs at ten cents a hundred. Incidentally, that money was used for the serious purpose of buying firecrackers to applaud the Founding Fathers on each Fourth of July." — Herbert Hoover

"I feel that I am one of his closest friends and he is one of my closest friends and that's the reason I am here. I am here because I like him, I'm here because I think he's doing the right thing in turning his documents over to the public here in this Library, and I am as happy as I can be to be a part of an organization that's here celebrating the birthday of one of America's greatest men, and I speak advisedly because I know most of them, and he's one of them." — Harry Truman

"That word America *carries meanings which lie deep in the soul of our people. ... It springs from our religious faith, our ideals of individual freedom and equal opportunity, which have come in the centuries since we landed on these shores. It rises from our pride in great accomplishments of our nation and from the sacrifices and devotion of those who have passed on. It lifts us above the ugliness of the day. It has guided us through even*

greater crises in our past. And from these forces, solutions will come again." — Herbert Hoover

Directions: From the North, take Interstate 380 south. Proceed east on Interstate 80 to Exit 254 (West Branch). Go 1/2 mile north to the Hoover Library-Museum at Parkside Drive and Main Street. From the East, travel I-80 west to the West Branch exit. Go 1/2 mile north to the library-museum. From the South, take Highway 218 north. Follow signs to I-80 east. Exit I-80 at West Branch, and go 1/2 mile north to the library-museum. From the West, travel I-80 east to the West Branch exit. Go 1/2 mile north to the library-museum.

Library-museum visitors enter through this glass door. *(Library-Museum)*

40

CHAPTER 5

THE CHAMP
FRANKLIN D. ROOSEVELT LIBRARY

(Franklin D. Roosevelt Library)

DESPAIR WAS FIRST MINIS-ter as America's 32nd president took the oath of office. On March 4, 1933, unemployment topped 13 million. Said outgoing President Herbert Hoover: "We are at the end of our string."

That April, writer Rud Rennie left Florida training camp to travel north with the New York Yankees. "We passed through southern cities which looked as though they had been ravaged by an invisible enemy," he said. "People seemed to be in hiding. They even would not come out to see Babe Ruth and Lou Gehrig."

More than 25 percent of America's workforce was out of work. In Wisconsin, farmers dumped milk on roads to reduce supply and lift prices. In Iowa, auctions halted because of bloody protests against foreclosure. Every state had either closed its banks or reduced their capacity to act. America seemed a cross between Dogpatch and Hades.

"First of all," the new president began his inaugural address, "let me reassert my firm belief that the only thing we have to fear is fear itself — nameless, unreasoning, unjustified terror." Did the seas part? No, but curtains opened.

Slowly, even self-awaredly, America as patient began to heal. From an unseen room burst the nation's shaman — "all grain and gusto," wrote Arthur Schlesinger, "but terribly hard inside ... who had been close enough to death to understand the frailty of human striving, but who remained loyal enough to life to do his best in the sight of God."

Even now, he elicits father of the New Deal and scourge of Nazi Germany — the man who created Social Security and hailed "my little dog Fala" and whom Adolf Hitler feared — his influence so huge — laughing, jousting, leading — that when he died on April 12, 1945, a part of each American died, too.

Once, conceding a salary larger than Hoover's, Babe Ruth explained: "But I had a better year than he did!" Most would tell you: not so with Franklin Delano Roosevelt.

LEAVE IT TO FDR TO BE PATRIcian, yet Falstaffian. He inherited wealth, graced Ivy League schools, and fought paralysis. He loved stamps, old movies, and pricking opponents. He was elected four times as president, served longer than any occupant, and transformed the office. He could not abide being pygmy in any way.

A Harvard graduate, Teddy Roosevelt's fifth cousin tripped from Woodrow Wilson's 1913-20 assistant Navy secretary to 1920 Democratic candidate for vice president — "I got to know the country as only a traveling salesman can" — to 1929-33 governor of New York. At 39, polio struck at FDR's summer home in Campabello off Canada. He was crippled, and changed, for life.

"You know," he later said, "I was an

The future 32nd president — before polio, the New Deal, and World War II. *(FDR Library)*

awfully mean cuss when I first went into politics." Polio softened FDR, made him seem more jaunty than arrogant. So did his wife, whom aide James Farley once called "the most practical woman I met in politics." Eleanor Roosevelt possessed a keen curiosity, soapbox mentality, and indiscriminate memory. One expected her to ford a stream, master a shotgun, or ward off the Indians till the cavalry came.

Already a nation-state, 1920s New York hailed a president in-the-making — the laugh, flung-back head, cigarette holder, exuberance, and rhetorical command. In 1928, FDR dubbed Al Smith "the Happy Warrior." In 1932, nominated for president, he said, "I pledge you, I pledge myself, to a New Deal for the American people." Its hub was Roosevelt. Its fount was what worked.

Each of America's 250 million-plus people has something central to his life. For Mario Cuomo, it is the immigrant experience. To George Bush, it was *noblesse oblige*; Adlai Stevenson, language-made-literate; Richard Nixon, the bruised tailbone of poverty. Roosevelt's next-to-polio central fact was that he would try anything. If it didn't fly, he tried something else.

Anything began the day after FDR's inaugural. He stopped gold transactions, called a national bank holiday, and hauled Congress into special session.

On March 9, Congress passed an array of presidential powers over banking. Would they work? Few knew. Roosevelt told son James, "All my life, I have been afraid of only one thing — fire. I think I'm afraid of something else — I may not have the strength to do this job."

Politics' fuel is trust. FDR ran on America's. He grasped that vivid, shorter, and personal were better. "People," Nixon said, "will give you 10 minutes before they turn to 'I Love Lucy.'" Roosevelt's was another medium. His born-for-radio voice turned heads. On March 12, 1933, he gave his first of 27 "Fireside Chats." He was a natural, and knew it: "My friends" ... "you and I" .... "we neighbors" made the complex simple, and drew you toward him. Segue to Ronald Reagan on 1980s television: block him, and he took to the air.

Six hundred banks had closed when FDR called it safe to store savings. The next day, doors opened in 12 Federal Reserve Bank cities and deposits swamped withdrawals. "The country needs and, unless I mistake its temper," he said, "the country demands persistent experimentation." It got it. It also got a broken-field runner who parried advice — pitting aides against one another — and touted public over private interest.

Congress adjourned June 15. By then, FDR had sent 15 separate proposals, and Congress passed all 15. He cut

When America attacked the Axis, economic might was her greatest ally. *(FDR Library)*

production via farm subsidies, ensured small-bank deposits, and began a pre-War on Poverty. Next came Social Security, unemployment insurance, Wall Street regulation, and collective bargaining. Acronyms lit Washington — CCC and AAA, SEC and FHA, CWA and FDIC. The Works Progress Administration (WPA) built hospitals, schools, and airports. The Tennessee Valley Authority (TVA) spun the kindly light and heat that led.

Critics scored FDR's "welfare state." Replied The Champ: "Government has a final responsibility for the well-being of its citizenship."

THE DIVIDE PRESAGED TRUMAN against "privilege," Carter *v.* corruption, and Reagan *v.* "welfare queens" — the president as national trustee *v.* real or fancied foil. FDR's was "economic royalists."

"I have earned the hatred of entrenched greed," he said, "and I welcome their hatred." The gentry returned his bile. FDR was "that man" — "a traitor to his class." Which did they resent most? How they devolved into fall guy, cemented FDR's link to the lower-middle class, or were impotent to respond? In 1936, Roosevelt carried 46 states to Alf Landon's two. "As Maine goes," jeered Farley, "so goes Vermont."

What a boxing match. In one corner, the rich as whipping boy; the other, what *TIME* called "Cleanser of the Temple." Consider FDR's antennae, personality, and art as imagery — "New Deal" — America's "rendezvous with destiny" — business' "industrial dictatorships" — the U.S. as "the great arsenal of democracy" — its "Four Freedoms" of speech, worship, and against want and fear. Tilting odds was Roosevelt's control of GOP-owned papers. Banning direct quote, he used newsmen to avoid boredom, convey a message, and stage a cheerful conspiracy against their editors. The fight should have been stopped on points.

Bonhomie was the effect, and aim. We thought of Eleanor — enduring is

Roosevelt speaking in New York. The Empire State was good to FDR. He carried it six times for governor and president. *(Ben Heller)*

known," Secretary of the Interior Ickes told him.

"Because I get too hard at times?"

"No," said Ickes, "you never get too hard but you won't talk frankly even with people of whose loyalty you are fully convinced. You keep your cards up close against your belly."

FDR told an aide, "You'll have to learn that public life takes a lot of sweat, but it doesn't need to worry you." Equanimity helped. Only Lincoln's crises matched FDR's. Labor strife. Wind and drought that buried farms under currents of sand. Tatters like Senator Huey Long, Dr. Francis Townsend, and Father Charles E. Coughlin. Angst leading people to doubt free enterprise itself. FDR took them on — and beat them all. Then, like earthquake spawning avalanche, his planet faced world war.

Roosevelt at cabinet meetings, noting what "my missus says" — and their children and Scotch terrier Fala as extended members of the family. Yet beyond that — what? It was hard to say that we knew the man who said grace around our table. "You are a wonderful person but you are one of the most difficult men to work with that I have

In his 1933 inaugural, FDR devoted one paragraph to events abroad. Were he to give that speech now, he said in 1937, most of it would etch foreign policy. Roosevelt's second term doubled the budget, tried to increase the size of the Supreme Court — his goal, reverse New Deal acts declared unconstitutional: Hoover called it "packing" — and sought to kick out Democratic conservatives. Yet history stops at another door.

FDR is judged a fine World War II leader. Many think him greater pre-war. Roosevelt had opposed intervention. "I have seen war," he said in 1936. "I have seen the agony of mothers and wives. I hate war." Adolf Hitler seized Austria. Neville Chamberlain chose appeasement. The Third Reich ate Czechoslovakia. By 1939, FDR knew that America must fight a war it feared, but the Axis had made inevitable.

"Never in my life," he wrote, "have I seen things moving in the world with more crosscurrents or greater velocity." On August 22, 1939, Hitler and Joseph Stalin signed the Russo-German Nonaggression Pact. Ten days later, German tanks crossed the Polish frontier. The oceans beside America were shrinking by the day.

HOLD THAT FACT AGAINST THE tone of 1939. Smaller than Bulgaria's, the U.S. Army practiced with wooden rifles. FDR's riposte: increase armament, and begin the greatest naval construction program since World War I. Militarily,

America was impotent. Roosevelt's problem was that Americans didn't care.

Most did by spring 1940. Nazi dominoes littered Norway and Denmark, the Low Countries and France. Italy declared war on France and Britain. "On this tenth day of June," said FDR, "the hand that held the dagger has stuck it into the back of its neighbor." At home, scales began to fall. Congress approved the sale of surplus war materiel to Britain. FDR transferred 50 overage destroyers, and cajoled Congress to resume the draft. That fall, a slogan went, "Roosevelt is not running against Wendell Willkie. He's running against Adolf Hitler." Winning a third term, he was also running against time. Only England deprived Hitler of "the abyss of a new Dark Age," said new Prime Minister Winston Churchill, "made more sinister, perhaps more protracted, by the lights of perverted science."

FDR's role in freedom's 1940-41 orbit incensed America's erect-a-wall/isolationist/avoid foreign entanglement heart.

Judge him duplicitous, decidedly unneutral, brilliant — and right. He did what great leaders do — show leadership, not followship — making America accomplice, then actor, in the seminal conflict of our age. In December 1940, Roosevelt lent arms to Britain on understanding that at war's end they would be returned or replaced. Soon, he defined the Atlantic Charter with Churchill, inked the Lend-Lease Act and occupied Greenland and Iceland, gave a $15 billion credit to Hitler's now-enemy, Stalin's Russia, and proclaimed unlimited national emergency.

In September 1941, a Nazi U-boat attacked the U.S. destroyer *Greer*. FDR told the Navy to shoot on sight. On December 7, sailors readied for the 8 A.M. flag-raising at Pearl Harbor. On the battleship *California*, Durell Connor wrapped Christmas gifts. A *West Virginia*'s mate studied photos from his wife of their eight-month-old son. The day af-

ter "a day that will live in infamy," FDR asked Congress to declare "war on the empire of Japan."

Roosevelt said, "The two madmen [Hitler and Mussolini] respect force and force alone." Force now let the U.S. redeem his pledge of February 18, 1942: "Soon we and not our enemies will have the offensive."

At Casablanca, FDR and Churchill demanded the Axis' "unconditional surrender." Cairo plotted strategem for the Pacific Theatre. Teheran appointed date and commander for the invasion of Normandy. Portending the United

The Champ, July 4, 1937, at Hyde Park. Recall "the laugh, flung-back head, cigarette holder, [and] exuberance," writes the author of FDR — to millions, the president still. *(UPI/Corbis-Bettman)*

Nations, it rested on British-American support. At the end of a cable FDR wrote Churchill, "It is fun to be in the same decade with you."

Exhausted and inexhaustible, Roosevelt bestrode World War II. Ask, and he received. Buy war bonds, grow "victory gardens," and donate more than 13 million pints of blood. Housewives bore shortages, and brooked food and gas rationing and citywide dimouts. FDR won a fourth term, traveled by warship and his plane, *The Sacred Cow*, and taunted the GOP. At a Teamsters Union dinner, Roosevelt denied that he had left his dog behind on the Aleutian Islands and sent a destroyer back to get him.

"These Republican leaders have not been content with attacks on me, or my wife, or on my sons," he said. "No, not content with that, they now include my little dog Fala." You needn't be a Democrat to toast the President for Life.

On D-Day, Roosevelt read a prayer over nationwide network radio. America, as community, and FDR, as parish minister, fused then, and evermore. In early 1945, he reported to Congress after dividing the post-war world in Yalta. For years a gentleman's agreement banned newsreels from showing him in a wheelchair. Now, too weary to stand, FDR sat in the chair, creased of face, his eyes pools of black. He looked like death — but you

Roosevelt was dying when he met Winston Churchill and Joseph Stalin at Yalta in early 1945. The trio discussed the European and Pacific Theatres and the post-war world. *(FDR Library)*

Franklin D. Roosevelt Library. Hyde Park, New York. Said FDR, fondly and poignantly, in 1941 as World War II approached: "This is a peaceful countryside." *(FDR Library)*

didn't worry. Surely, Roosevelt was not about to die.

ON APRIL 12, AT HIS HOME IN Warm Springs, Georgia, FDR suffered a cerebral hemorrhage. Said Robert Taft, "He literally worked himself to death on behalf of the American people." Returning from war, soldiers would confront old, unfamiliar places. No change stunned more than President Harry S. Truman.

"One remembers Roosevelt as a kind of smiling bus driver, with cigarette holder pointed upward, listening to the uproar from behind as he took the sharp turns," Samuel Grafton wrote. "They used to tell him that he had not loaded his vehicle right for all eternity. But he knew he had it stacked well enough to round the next corner and he knew when the

yells were false and when they were real, and he loved the passengers."

FDR was not Ralph Kramden, nor the United States the Brooklyn MTA. It is enough that America did not feel insecure. We did not feel diminished. We could do anything, and did — oust Depression, crush tyranny, make ours the planet's "sun, moon, and stars." FDR had that way.

Some call his legacy how for millions the term president still means Roosevelt. Others, that he changed America so fiercely that 10 successors — many trying — have not changed her back. FDR left what he sought, and loved. His America never felt puny, or afraid.

Franklin D. Roosevelt Library. Verne W.

★ ★ WINDOWS ON THE WHITE HOUSE ★ ★

Roosevelt's desk in the Oval Office, replete with mementoes and bric-a-brac. The library keeps it much as it was the day FDR died — April 12, 1945. *(Photo-Creations)*

Newton, Director. 511 Albany Post Road, Hyde Park, New York 12538-1999. Phone: (914) 229-8114. Fax: (914) 229-0872. Web site: http://www.academic.marist.edu/FDR.

Visitors have included: Presidents Truman, Kennedy, Johnson, Nixon, and Clinton. Vice President Henry Wallace. Soviet Premier Nikita Khrushchev. Ethiopian Emperor Haile Selassie. The Duke of Kent. Supreme Court Justice Felix Frankfurter. Senators George McGovern and Daniel Moynihan. Governors Michael Dukakis, W. Averell Harriman, and Nelson Rockefeller. Mayor Fiorello LaGuardia. General William Westmoreland. Broadcasters David

Brinkley and Dave Garroway. Actors Douglas Fairbanks, Jr., Paul Newman, Edward G. Robinson, and Cicely Tyson. Singer Marian Anderson. Playwright Arthur Miller.

Hours: Daily, 9 A.M. to 5 P.M. November through April. Daily, 9 A.M. to 6 P.M. May through October. Open every day, except New Year's Day, Thanksgiving, and Christmas. Admission: Children age 15 years and under, school groups, and seniors over 62, free. Golden Eagle and Golden Age passports honored. Age 16 to 61, $4. Group tours are urged in advance of trip to call (914) 229-9115. For research information, details on educational programs, and reservations for educational groups, call (914) 229-8114. Free parking. Library gift shop is open during regular hours.

★ ★ ★

"HALF-A-CENTURY AGO, A SMALL boy took especial delight in combing an old tree, now unhappily gone, to pick and eat ripe Seckel pears," a large man said on November 19, 1939 at Hyde Park, New York. "That was one hundred feet to the west of where we stand ... In the spring of the year, in hip rubber boots, he sailed his first toy boats in the surface water formed by the melting snows. In the summer, with his dogs, he dug into the woodchuck holes of this same field. The descendants of those same wood-chucks still inhabit the field, and I hope they will continue to for all time."

Woodchucks still thrive a half-century after Franklin Roosevelt presided over the laying of his library cornerstone. FDR's was conceived April 12, 1937. His sketch shows a plan similar to today's building, and location portending its ultimate site. Forward to December 10, 1938. He invited scholars, educators, and public-opinion analysts to the White House. How to keep material "whole and intact ... in one ... locality?" In part, through adding to Roosevelt's the papers and artifacts of past and current aides in Albany and Washington.

Work began on the building in fall 1939. What irony for the foil of "economic royalists"! FDR built it with pri-

In 1944, Roosevelt said, "All that is within me cries out to go back to my home on the Hudson River." See why in this library exhibit on FDR's youth. *(FDR Library)*

FDR's Hyde Park study, where he spoke by radio to America. "My friends, you and I" — he said, and suddenly the land was whole. Note wheelchair, left. *(FDR Library)*

vately donated funds, at a cost of $376,000, and gave it to the government on July 4, 1940. At the time, Robert D.W. Connor, the archivist of the United States, observed, "Franklin D. Roosevelt is the nation's answer to the historian's prayer." Said FDR in 1941: "This is a peaceful countryside, and it seems appropriate that in this time of strife we should dedicate the library to the spirit of peace — peace for the United States and soon, we hope, peace for the world."

A year before, Roosevelt gained a *nonpareil* third term. Soon, his became the only presidential library used by a sitting president. Wartime guests included King George VI of Great Britain and Prime Minister Winston Churchill. FDR gave four "fireside chats" from his Hyde Park study, and the last speech of his fourth campaign for president on November 6, 1944. "He always felt that this was his home," said Eleanor, "and he loved the house and the view, the woods, special trees..."

Special was a trait even Republicans affixed to FDR. You see and feel it at his 188-acre boyhood home.

FORTY-SIX THOUSAND VISITORS toured Roosevelt's estate in fiscal year 1942. Its subject paid his last visit at Easter 1945. By 1947, 304,526 flocked to the park and saw his grave in the rose garden. A few steps away, the library was completed in 1972 with the north and south wings — the Eleanor Roosevelt Addition. Was FDR a Nostradamus? In 1942, his sketches prophesied the need for extra space — addition to the original block in the style of Hudson Valley fieldstone.

"Roosevelt was eclectic," observed library director Verne Newton. "He loved architecture, and understood family, place, and country. He was a hobbyist, and collected books on history, economics, government, public affairs, and travel. Samuel Eliot Morison put it best when he said, 'If Franklin Roosevelt had never become president, he still would have gone down in history as one of the great collectors.'" Standing near the family home, you recall how in 1944 FDR briefly deferred a fourth term in office. "All that is within me," he said, "cries out to go back to my home on the Hudson River."

Herbert Hoover had received about 400 letters a day at the White House. That was not unusual. Americans rarely wrote to a president. Roosevelt was different. Daily, they sent him as many as 4,000 letters. "Dear Mr. President," read one, "I can't get along on my WPA allowance." Another: "Dear Mr. President, that was a wonderful speech on the radio last night." In time, Roosevelt — "the good soldier," he called himself — succumbed to re-election. Hyde Park sug-

Few Americans even realized that their president was disabled. One reason: FDR's 1936 Ford "Phaeton," which let him drive the car with special hand controls. *(FDR Library)*

Eleanor Roosevelt — to Adlai Stevenson, "First Lady of the World." (*FDR Library*)

gests why. "Dear Mr. President," a letter reads, "my son is only a private in the Army. He needs you to become a major."

By 1945, Roosevelt's papers filled almost 500 five-drawer cabinets. Today, over 200 collections, totaling more than 17 million pages, are housed in his library. They include the papers of Mrs. Roosevelt — by her 1962 death, three million-plus pages — and members of the Roosevelt and Delano families and close associates, including Secretary of the Treasury Henry Morgenthau, Jr.,

Special Assistant Harry L. Hopkins, and aides Adolf Berle and Rexford Tugwell. Beside manuscripts, the library boasts 44,000 volumes, including FDR's personal library of 15,000 books and pamphlets.

"Scholars and laymen come here," said Newton. "You can be either, and leave feeling you know the man." To wit, FDR's books on Naval and Dutchess County history, British and American literature, and ornithology. Audiovisuals of sound recordings, 700 reels of motion picture film, and 130,000 still photographs from portraits to candid shots. Guests play the games "Secret Agents in the Oval Office" or "Touch the Presidency" and learn of FDR's love of stamps.

"When Hyde Park was first suggested," the director continued, "some said, 'The Library of Congress was good enough for Washington and Jefferson. Why not put FDR's papers there?'" The question seems lunatic — they *belong* here — as the sun sets on FDR's dreamstuff soil of back country and small shops and lyric Dutch names.

PRE-FDR, PRESIDENTS AND THEIR families rarely supplied open access to presidential papers. By 1950, 85 percent of FDR's personal and public papers were opened to research. They included: Albert Einstein's August 2, 1939 letter to

After FDR's death, Eleanor Roosevelt lived in two homes — Val-Kill Cottage in Hyde Park and an apartment in New York (above). This display shows her place of work. *(Photo-Creations)*

Roosevelt on nuclear weapons; a 1943 map of General George Patton's showing the U.S. Seventh Army's drive to capture Sicily; and FDR's October 20, 1944 missive to General Douglas MacArthur hailing his successful beachhead in the Philippine Islands.

Pack rat, or visionary? Roosevelt saved correspondence from the time he entered public life. Reading, you hail his mother, who stashed each letter that he wrote to her and things from school essays to history tests. He embraced her taste — a love of the Navy, and Hudson Valley — and preserved books, cartoons,

scrimshaw, and sleighs. "And while he was attending to his own special interests," Newton said, "friends, admirers, and foreign dignitaries gave him objects to mark his presidency — cigarette holders, canes, bejeweled daggers, swords, cathedrals made of toothpicks, ancient leather texts — and other articles that he discreetly called 'oddities.'" You see them hard by the Hudson River. Franklin Roosevelt, Superstar.

FDR greets you with the desk that he used from 1933-45. Notice its melange of figurework — Republican elephants, and Democratic donkeys — unchanged

"Sail On, O Ship of State." Roosevelt was Woodrow Wilson's assistant Navy secretary. Notice FDR's beloved hat, cane, and cape as part of the museum's "America on the Seas" exhibit. *(FDR Library)*

since his death. What strikes a visitor is the number of gifts for him and Mrs. Roosevelt from abroad-and-here admirers. Like mail, this lacked precedent. "Hundreds of things came in each day," recalled Newton, "ranging from paper weights to cakes and hams. Beyond that, there were the valuables — diamonds, jewelry, fine glassware, luggage and other things of that sort that started coming to the White House en masse." Many grace the halls of what Roosevelt, not wanting to honor himself, called the "Hyde Park Library."

Ironically, FDR personalized the presidency more than Ike, Johnson, Nixon, or even Lincoln. Hyde Park reflects it. See Roosevelt's 1936 Ford Phaeton with special hand controls to let him drive the roads of Sleepy Hollow; "The First Fifty Years" gallery of his youth, schooling, and career through the 1932 presidential nomination; and "America on the Seas," an exhibit of FDR's memorabilia on the U.S. sailing navy. A visitor sees photos of faces seared by Great Depression; an umbrella of New Deal measures debated then, and now; and the study that Roosevelt designed and loved.

CLOUGH OBSERVED, "WESTWARD, look, the land is bright." It seems fluorescent trooping to the Eleanor Roosevelt Gallery.

You will enjoy the film biography, copy of part of her post-FDR New York City apartment, display of her bequest to the U.S. and United Nations — and grasp why Adlai Stevenson called her "First Lady of the World." Then, walk to the farewell gallery, where "Dr. New Deal" becomes "Dr. Win the War."

Newton observed, "The majority of our visitors grew up with Roosevelt. The library brings it all back — their youth, and lives since. People leave, and you hear them comparing FDR to successors, mostly in his favor. Many have tears in their eyes. There's nostalgia, melancholy, and reverence — especially in the war gallery where our entire century changed."

World War II exhibits feature a video, copy of the secret "Map Room" — the wartime White House basement communications center — and interactive displays that let a visitor play general or admiral and direct the Allied Forces. The war's turning points complete the area — Midway, say, or Stalingrad, or America-at-home as "the great arsenal of democracy."

In 1991-95, World War II history weekends lured thousands of visitors to Hyde Park. They recalled a time of crossroad, unknown, and names like Remagen, El Alamein, and Guadalcanal. Espy the "Commander in Chief" exhibit — you decide the fate of Britain — or "Presidential Years" display. Like that, you recall Bataan, Normandy, and the Battle of the Bulge.

In the Hudson Valley, forget Tolstoy. *War and Peace* remains FDR's bequest.

Dedication excerpts, June 30, 1941.

"Among democracies, I think through all the recorded history of the world, the building of the permanent institutions like libraries and museums for the use of all the people flourishes. And that is especially true in our own land, because we believe that people ought to work out for themselves, and through their own study, the determination of their best interest rather than accept such so-called information as may be handed out to them by certain types of self-constituted leaders who decide what is best for them." — Franklin D. Roosevelt

"This particular Library is but one of many new Libraries. And so, because it happens to be a national one, I as President have the privilege of accepting this newest house in which people's records are preserved — public papers and collections that refer to our own period of history. And this latest addition to the archives of America is dedicated at a moment when government of the people by themselves is being attacked everywhere." — FDR

★ ★ WINDOWS ON THE WHITE HOUSE ★ ★

"As all of you know, into this Library has gone, and will continue to go, the interest and loving care of a great many people. Most of you who are here today are old friends and neighbors of mine — friends and neighbors throughout the years. And so all of you, my friends and neighbors, are in a sense Trustees of this Library through the years to come." — FDR

"I think that the ceremonies are now over, except for one very important addition that relates to the future. Under an Act of the Congress of the United States, there was authorized to be appointed a Board of Trustees, who will be responsible for this Library from midnight tonight, through the years to come. I am glad that you have come today, because as I suggested at lunch to some of the Trustees, this is the last chance you have got to see this Library free of charge. At *midnight tonight the Government of the United States takes over."* — FDR

Directions: From the North, take Interstate 87 (New York State Thruway) south to Exit 18 at New Paltz. Follow Route 299 east to Route 9 south. Cross the Mid-Hudson Bridge to Route 9 north. The Roosevelt Library is on the left side of Route 9, four miles north of Poughkeepsie. From the East, go west on Interstate 84. Proceed north on Highway 9 to the library. From the South, take the Taconic Parkway to Route 84 west. Follow 84 to Route 9 north. The library is on the left side, four miles north of Poughkeepsie. From the West, travel east on I-84 across the Newburgh-Beacon Bridge to Route 9 north. Go north on Highway 9 to the library.

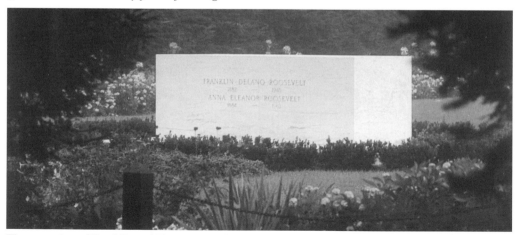

The gravesites of Franklin and Eleanor Roosevelt (1882-1945 and 1884-1962, respectively), planted with myrtle, lie in front of the white marble monument which FDR designed. *(FDR Library)*

CHAPTER 6

A TOUCH OF HARRY
HARRY S. TRUMAN LIBRARY

(U.S. Navy)

"I STILL HAVE DIFFICULTY," A critic wrote in 1978, "seeing John F. Kennedy clear." By contrast, a certain predecessor left almost nothing to the imagination. America's 33rd president was a bespectacled 5-foot-9 machine protégé with poor sight and grand vision. Speaker of the House Sam Rayburn termed him "right on all the big things, wrong on most of the little ones." Color Harry Truman pugnacious, hyperbolic, pygmy, and gargantuan.

Returning after World War I to his hometown of Independence, Missouri, Truman married fifth-grade sweetheart Elizabeth Wallace and became a Kansas City clothier. His partner was Eddie Jacobson. The two had run an Army post canteen, but their new thread turned bare. At 38, Truman was broke, and in debt.

The Commander in Chief and Mrs. Truman enjoy the Army-Navy football game in Philadelphia. Truman's eyesight made him more a sports spectator than participant. *(Harry S. Truman Library)*

To the rescue: Tom Pendergast, a Missouri political boss, who helped elect him to a 1922 district judgeship. Truman made the U.S. Senate and vice presidency, respectively, in 1934 and '44.

"Who the hell is Harry Truman!?" Admiral William Leahy, White House chief of staff, asked Franklin Roosevelt in the summer of 1944. Response links the terms decent, self-confident, unhandsome, and unknown — by turn/taste a singsong speaker, rank dresser, and vestibule of Mid-America — artillery captain in France, Shriner, Eagle, and member of the Baptist Church.

"We chose Truman [as Roosevelt's third veep, replacing Henry Wallace]," an FDR aide confessed, "because he was from a Border State and all of us were tired." He could laugh at himself, and hated phonies. So what if he seemed unpresidential? We weren't picking a president. Some people impress you most the first time you meet them. Truman grew on you, like the bourbon he loved playing poker.

On April 12, 1945, Truman ended a dry day presiding over the Senate by joining Rayburn for a drink. The White House switchboard found him there and ordered him across town. Arriving, Truman heard numbing news. Mrs. Roosevelt confirmed it: "Harry, the president is dead." Was there anything he could do for her? Truman asked. She said, "Is there anything we can do for you? For you are the one in trouble now."

Hallo to America's Little Touch of Harry in the Night.

LATER, *THE NEW YORK TIMES*' Cabell Phillips recalled the reaction to FDR's death: "Good God, Truman will be president."

After shock, irony. The first impression *v.* Roosevelt was of contrast, not succession.

John Dos Passos called FDR's "the patroon voice, the headmaster's admonition, the bedside doctor's voice that spoke to ... all of us." Truman's was flat, and high. Roosevelt dressed to the manor born. Harry wore double-breasted suits with two-toned wingtip shoes. FDR scent of big-league. Truman seemed out of his. Olympian, Roosevelt fought disability. Rotarian, Harry fought a shroud of bumbling. "To err is Truman," jibed sophists. "I'm just mild about Harry." It was said that FDR saved capitalism for the capitalists. Who foretold Churchill's saw: "No one more saved western civilization than Harry Truman"?

A day after FDR's death, Truman told reporters, "Boys, if you ever pray, pray for me now." For a time, you prayed to history. Hitler shot himself. After FDR's death, Truman first learned of nuclear tests — and that an invasion of Japan might cost a million casualties. On July 26, 1945, he told her to surrender or face ruin. Spurned, Truman ordered the B-29 *Enola Gay* to drop the first atomic bomb. On September 2, Douglas MacArthur signed the surrender document: "We have had our last chance. If we do not devise some greater and more equitable system, Armageddon will be at our door."

Confusion was soon at Truman's. On one hand, his home policy had a deep identity — civil rights, national health insurance, and government pledge of a decent standard of living. On the other, impatience was his unwelcome guest. What a repast! America had beat the Nazis. Where was her dessert — goods and housing? The first post-war year fused shortage, price control, rising prices, the black market, and 107,476 man-hours lost to strikes. Truman's "Fair Deal" hoped to build on FDR's beginnings. Its more immediate task was to meet pent-up demand.

Abroad, the demand pertained to tryanny. The Soviets domineered Eastern Europe. The Grand Alliance sought their retreat. At first liking Stalin — "Uncle Joe" — Truman soon tongue-lashed his foreign minister. "I have never been talked to like that in my life," huffed

Churchill, Truman, and Stalin meet at Potsdam in 1945. The summit shed scales from Truman's eyes: Stalin became less "Uncle Joe" than a despot bent on subjugation. *(U.S. Navy)*

V.M. Molotov. "Carry out your agreements," Truman said, "and you won't ...!" The Red Armies occupied Poland and much of Germany. Truman was helpless, and hated it. "I'm tired," he wrote, "of babying the Soviets."

Churchill never tried: "From Stettin in the Baltic to Trieste in the Adriatic an Iron Curtain has descended across the continent." Like Truman, he was dead before the curtain finally lifted.

LATER, HERBERT AGAR WROTE, "During the next few years this strange little man — lively and pert to the verge of bumptiousness; more widely read in history than any President since John Quincy Adams; more willful than any President since James K. Polk; more incompetent in dividing the good from the bad among his own friends at home than any President since Warren Harding — would make and enforce a series of decisions upon which, for better or for worse, our world now rests, or shakes."

Truman was a gambler who bet the ranch, seldom second-guessed himself, and often won the pot. In 1947, Britain cut off aid to Greece and Turkey. Communism held the cards, but Truman refused to fold. In March, he asked Congress for $400 million in aid. On June 5, Secretary of State George Marshall proposed a plan of aid to nations which helped rebuild Western Europe. In 1948, Stalin curbed Western traffic into Berlin, 110 miles behind the Iron Curtain, and blockaded railways to starve its non-Russian sectors. Would the U.S. respond? An airlift fed Berlin for 321 days before the Russians had enough.

"*Had* enough?" Republicans had already asked. For the first time since 1928, they won control of both houses of Congress. Forget Rayburn's "big things"; Truman seemed, well, so pedestrian.

Daughter Margaret debuted as a professional singer at Consitution Hall. A *The Washington Post* critic wrote that she "communicates almost nothing of the music." Truman hit the roof. "I have just seen your lousy review of Margaret's concert," he wrote. "Some day I hope to meet you ... You'll need a new nose, a lot of beefsteak for black eyes, and perhaps a supporter below."

Near Fulton, Missouri, he donned an engineer's cap and drove the locomotive. In Kansas City, he visited a barbershop: "None of that fancy stuff. I don't want anything that smells." Harry dubbed wife Bess "the boss," termed visitors "the

"The Buck Stops Here" sign adorns Truman's desk in the re-created Oval Office. Atop the desk, among other things, are a baseball, lucky horseshoe, and Democratic donkey. *(Truman Library)*

customers," took his daily "constitutional," and had a sign on his desk, "The Buck Stops Here." "If you can't stand the heat," he said, "get out of the kitchen." Truman could, and rarely did.

In 1945, a reporter first called him Mr. President. He said, "I wish you didn't have to call me that." By 1948, most Americans agreed. A Gallup Poll said that Truman would lose to Republicans Stassen, MacArthur, Vandenberg, or Thomas E. Dewey. Said GOP Congresswoman Clare Boothe Luce: "Truman is a gone goose."

Deluded: the '48 Republican nominee. The Democrats had split into Progressive and States Rights (Dixiecrats) parties: their nominees, respectively, Henry Wallace and Strom Thurmond. The inheritor — "an authentic colossus," Lowell Thomas said — behaved as though coronated. How could Dewey lose?

Dismissed: the incumbent — "Give 'em Hell, Harry" — who believed with a Tooth Fairy kind of surety. The 80th Congress spurned Social Security and minimum wage legislation and passed the Taft-Hartley Act, which labor hated. Truman saw a wedge: Was Congress guardian of your purse or a tribune of privilege?

Evoked: Truman's tongue, and America's ardor for the underdog. "If you send another Republican Congress to Washington," he stormed, "you're a bigger bunch of suckers than I think you are." Dewey became the "front man" endorsing Hitler, Tojo, and Mussolini — the GOP "gluttons of privilege ... bloodsuckers" who "stuck a pitcher in every farmer's back." Was Truman spunky, or hysterical? The odds against him rose to 15-1.

ON OCTOBER 11, *NEWSWEEK* READ, "Fifty political experts unanimously predict a Dewey victory." Truman told aides, "Oh, those damned fellows, they're always wrong, anyway." Dewey, crowing, said, "Remember, when you're ahead, don't talk."

On Election Day, Truman drove to a resort 30 miles from Independence and checked into a hotel. By 8 P.M. he was asleep. In the exterior world, a *Chicago Tribune* headline — "Dewey Defeats Truman!" — prophesied the farm vote, Republican since McKinley. At midnight, Truman awoke, turned the radio on, and heard H.V. Kaltenborn say that though he led by 1.2 million votes, he was "undoubtedly beaten." Truman went back to sleep.

The farm vote began trickling in. Its coming was a false alarm: Dewey carried only seven states between the Alleghenies and the Pacific. Slowly, the GOP bent changed from surety to surprise, said Associated Press, "surprise to

The Himalaya of political upsets. Truman's good luck was the *Chicago Tribune*'s misfortune. The morning after, Harry revels in its headline: "Dewey Defeats Truman." *(Truman Library)*

doubt, from doubt to disbelief, and then on to stunned fear and panic."

Assuming victory, the GOP Congress had appropriated a record $100,000 for the inaugural. Truman spent it. He and Republicans then made 1949-53 a political no-man's land. On September 23, 1949, the Soviets exploded an A-bomb. In June 1950, Truman took to television to announce war in Korea. Former official Alger Hiss was charged with giving secret documents to Russia, found guilty of perjury, and sentenced to five years in jail. Truman called the case a "red herring." He was wrong. Hiss was a spy.

Who lost China? Truman, said the GOP. Marshall's successor, Dean Acheson, replied: "The Nationalist [Chinese] Armies did not have to be defeated; they disintegrated." In February 1950, U.S. atomic scientist Klaus Fuchs was arrested for giving the Soviets atomic secrets. "Fuchs and Acheson and Hiss and hydrogen bombs threatening outside and New Dealism eating away the vitals of the nation," scalded Senator Homer Capehart. "In the name of Heaven, is this the best America can do?"

U.N. Commander Douglas MacArthur asked, too. On March 24, 1951, he issued a statement urging Truman to attack Red China's "coastal areas and

An Oval Office reproduction from the early 1950s. Portraits on the wall were gifts from Venezuela, Argentina, and Mexico. The globe was given to Truman by General Eisenhower. *(Truman Library)*

interior bases." The president refused; he wanted a Korean truce. MacArthur wanted China's demise, and said so in an April 5 letter to GOP House leaders. It was the last straw. Truman sacked him for insubordination.

Truman was booed at Griffith Stadium. Flags flew at half-mast. On April 19, MacArthur told Congress how a ballad of his youth "proclaimed that 'old soldiers never die, they just fade away.'" Truman was burned in effigy. Flags now flew upside down.

"I'M GOING TO HAVE A TRUMAN beer," the joke went, "just like any beer except that it hasn't got a head." Millions of Americans called for Truman's impeachment. Avenging Dewey, the Congressional GOP went squarely for the jugular — its shorthand, K1C2: Korea, corruption, and Communism. In 1951-53, Truman's Gallup Poll approval dropped to 23 percent, and never rose over 32.

Truman was right on Korea, Berlin, MacArthur, and the Marshall Plan. He floundered on the personal. Dwight Eisenhower was "a phony." Richard Nixon became "a lying son of a bitch." When Dewey died in 1971, he refused to issue a condolence. Trenching himself in fiat, Truman viewed politics bluntly and stubbornly — unforgiving and unself-conscious, without pretense or balm.

The statesman, not partisan, was more attractive then and now. In 1952, he gave his 300th press conference. "I have tried my best to give the Nation everything I have in me," Truman confided. "There are a great many people — I suppose a million in this country — who could have done the job better than I did it. But I had the job and I had to do it. I always quote an epitaph which is in the cemetery at Tombstone, Arizona. It says: 'Here lies Jack Williams. He done his damndest.'"

There are worse ways to be recalled.

Harry S. Truman Library. Larry Hackman, Director. U.S. Highway 24 and Delaware, Independence, Missouri 64050-1798. Phone: (816) 833-1400. Fax: (816) 833-4368. Web site: Library at Truman.narra.gov.

Visitors have included: Presidents Hoover, Eisenhower, Kennedy, and Nixon. First Ladies Eleanor Roosevelt and Pat Nixon. Prime Minister Margaret Thatcher. Senator John Glenn. Coretta Scott King. Broadcaster Edward R. Murrow. Actors Jack Benny, Paul Newman, and Ginger Rogers.

Harry S. Truman Library. Independence, Missouri. Some wanted it to salute Truman's life. He declined, believing that monuments should not honor a living person. *(Truman Library)*

This copy of the Liberty Bell was given by the City of Annecy-Le-Vieux, France. *(Jeff Brooks)*

Hours: Daily, 9 A.M. to 5 P.M. Open every day, except New Year's Day, Thanksgiving, and Christmas. (Research room hours, Monday through Friday, 8:45 A.M. to 4:45 P.M. Closed on federal holidays.) Admission: Children age 15 years and under, and students in organized group tours for whom application has been made in advance, free. Others, $2. Free parking. Library gift shop is open during regular hours.

IT IS SAID THAT AFTER LEAVING the White House, Harry Truman once came into his living room to discover wife Bess tossing their old love letters into the fireplace.

"Think of history!" said a horrified Truman.

Said Bess: "I have."

As a boy, Truman read Homer's *Ulysses*, Lytton's *The Last Days of Pompeii*, and about the civilizations of Egypt, Greece, and Mesopotamia. Leaving the presidency in 1953, he tried to apply their lode to his papers and future library. Its lessons, he believed, could buoy America.

Truman wanted his papers used by heartland students and scholars, and near him for easy reference: memoirs, after all. Too, the Roosevelt Library had become a hit. Truman noticed. He wanted his papers and other materials kept together in one place, and used by historians in the near, not murky, future. So return them to Missouri, open them as soon as possible, and create a nonprofit corporation to raise money for a library.

Founded in 1950, the corporation's trustees included Eleanor Roosevelt, George Marshall, and Dean Acheson. Questions daunted. Where to build? The front-runner was Grandview, Missouri, where Truman once worked the family farm. Other bidders included the University of Kansas City and the University of Missouri.

Truman liked a link to academe. Luckily for Independence, he liked his hometown more. On December 31, 1954, the Truman Library Corporation accepted its offer of 13 acres of parkland for the library.

Next, money and design. Truman cracked the former by speaking at fundraisers across the country. The latter produced a long, low building that paralleled the land. Groundbreaking occurred May 8, 1955, Truman's 71st birthday. In August, the Presidential Libraries Act, which let the government accept Truman's and future libraries, was signed into law. On July 6, 1957, the lot, library, and historic material became America's. Among other things, the U.S. gained a salient portico, site of gray Indiana limestone, and 70,000-square-foot interior.

Truman loved the research room, exhibit area, office suite for himself and staff, and stacks that could house more than 15 million pages. He evolved into the library's challenge/champion. How could a building reflect, well, the Andrew Jackson of our age? "I want to say,

you youngsters," he once said, "you'd better start studying the Presidency of the United States and how it works because one of you one of these days will be President of the United States, but I wouldn't advise you to try to be because if you ever get there you'll be sorry — the happiest day I ever spent ... was the day I left the White House."

Pause for breath. "They tried to kick me out but they didn't succeed in 1948. If they hadn't done that, I might have quit then, but whenever anybody tries to run over me he finds out he's got something to run over and that's all there is to it."

Finis. God broke the mold before He made Harry Truman.

Post-White House, Truman turned from making to reading history. He used this Independence office from 1957-72 — consuming books and greeting presidents from Hoover to Nixon. *(Truman Library)*

Thomas Hart Benton was President Truman's favorite artist. Today, his famed mural, "Independence and the Opening of the West," accents the library lobby. *(Truman Library)*

WHAT MOLDS SHAPED THE Truman Library? First, Truman "had arranged," Chief Justice Earl Warren said by way of dedicating it, "for the preservation of his papers in this library in such manner that his administration will be one of the 'clearest ages' of history."

Truman's papers then numbered more than five million. Their initial public opening was May 11, 1959. "It can certainly be claimed, as a contribution to the 'right to know,'" the library director wrote, "that a large part [90-plus percent] of ... [Truman's] papers opened only six years after the end of his administration."

Next, the library enjoyed the treasure/task of consulting a living former president. The National Archives had asked a local museum curator to choose the first exhibits. His plan focused on Truman's life. Harry hated it. "If the Truman Library in Independence had been conceived as a memorial to me personally," he later said, "I would have done everything I could to prevent its establishment during my lifetime ... I do not believe that monuments ... should be erected to a living person."

What he believed was that the presidency embraced six jobs. 1) The chief executive. 2) Ceremonial chief of staff. 3) Congress' partner in creating and passing legislation. 4) Director of the nation's foreign policy. 5) Commander in Chief of the Armed Forces. 6) Head of his political party. The offshoot was a display of presidential powers as listed in Article II of the Constitution, and areas of photos and documents of past administrations borrowed from the archives. To Truman, the office rededicated America as a winnowing force for good.

"Truman was extremely partisan," said former acting library director George Curtis. "Remember the statement he made at the '48 convention, 'We're going to beat those Republicans, and make them like it.' [He did. They didn't.] Yet he appointed to the board of

his library Republican Warren and asked him and Herbert Hoover to speak at the dedication." In 1957, Hoover hailed "Mr. Truman's generosity [which] has opened a large and important contribution to a period of American history to our people." His generosity, like other former presidents', included time.

Truman came to his office almost every working day. He prepared speeches, answered letters, welcomed guests, held meetings with old friends — and attended to his library. "Often, a museum staffer'd call Truman in a meeting and say, 'Some kids are here, and they want you to speak to them,'" said Curtis' successor, director Larry Hackman. "No

Daily, Truman took a walk — his "constitutional" — through downtown Washington. Riding, he took this 1950 Lincoln Cosmopolitan designed for the White House limousine fleet. *(Truman Library)*

appointment, but no problem. He spoke to them."

Truman recessed the meeting, and took guests to the auditorium. "He'd talk to maybe four student groups a day — always with the same message, 'study your history.'"

Knowing it, he loved its wonder — and hoped to impart the lessons of ancient Greece and Rome.

A LIBRARY MUST MAKE HISTORY a cross-generation crossing point, tying millions the way news of a young boy's first deer once linked tribal members. Enter 1990s technology to bring Truman's legacy to life for those to whom the Fair Deal seems paleozoic. The library enlisted PRESIDENT database, accessible through the internet, to enter its holdings. It also began a $10 million fundraising campaign that spawned two new galleries — the 2,000-square foot "White House Gallery" and 8,000-square foot "Presidential Gallery."

The "White House Gallery" opened in November 1995, and includes a video, three portraits, and full-scale reproduction of the Oval Office. Also, a TV monitor of presidents' lives like Washington and Lincoln — display cases of the original "The Buck Stops Here" sign on Truman's desk — "The President's Day": documents, pictures of visitors, and an appointment schedule of a typical Truman day — and "Dear Mr. President" letters from household names and Average Joes. Unhappy over taxes, one man mailed Truman the shirt off his back. Others mailed bags of cinders. A coal strike lit their match.

The "Presidential Gallery" will augment current bric-a-brac, boast interactive video, and open by late 1998. "Our goal is Truman's — to make this not just a great resource center, but a great educational center," observed Hackman. "That's especially true for young people, which means linking history to today and letting them participate. In 1996, we had a voting booth related to '48. First, you chose among Bill Clinton, Bob Dole, and Ross Perot — then, Truman, Dewey, Thurmond, and Wallace. Kids loved it."

Connecting tissue means changing temporary exhibits to shore the permanent stock. Among the latter to survive renovation: a large mural in the entrance lobby ("Independence and the Opening of the West" by Thomas Hart Benton), model of the Battleship U.S.S. *Missouri*, built during World War II for training purposes, and Truman's retirement office viewed from the library's courtyard. (Also in the courtyard are the graves of President and Mrs. Truman.)

"With the hoopla about [the half-century remembrance of] World War II, interest returned to Truman," said Hackman. "Yet each year fewer people are alive who remember that time. That's why we're updating the library. We want people who don't have an interest in Truman per se to react like his contemporaries. They will if the present relates to the man. You hear older visitors talk about Bataan, MacArthur's firing, or 1948. But beyond that, they focus on the same things — Truman's character. Honesty. Decisiveness. Everyone can understand those traits."

Visitors also grasp the solitary glory — or glorious misery? — of decision-making. "Over the last few years, we've received many comments about the end of World War II. People ask whether Truman was right to drop the A-bomb.

More than 99 percent of people come up and say, 'Of course he was.'"

SHAKESPEARE PENNED "TIDES IN the affairs of men." Truman's again flowed at the golden anniversary of his inheriting the presidency. In 1993, an exhibition on the American homefront during the Second World War — "Day of Infamy: War Comes to America" — re-created a small American town, and showed 1941-45 film, radiocast, and factory machinery. A National Archives exhibit — "World War II: Personal Accounts, Pearl Harbor to V-J Day," by Don Wilson, then-archivist of the United States, and LBJ curator Gary Yarrington

The library courtyard bears the gravesites of Mr. and Mrs. Truman. "Everybody in life should have a boss like I did," Harry said of Bess. They started courting in the fifth grade. *(Truman Library)*

— used letters, diaries, photographs, and mementoes to daub privates and generals in a world at war.

A more pacific, as opposed to Pacific, theatre housed "Greta Kempton's Palette: A Painter's World." Kempton was called the "court painter of the Truman Administration," and did President and Mrs. Truman's official White House portraits. Atop the temporary exhibit hit parade was a real parade on July 4, 1994 in Independence. It starred Truman's grandson, Clifton Truman Daniel, and a name change: The Truman Library was now called "The Truman" — as populist as its namesake.

The library has remained open during renovation. Completed, it will show a man still put to purpose against a new backdrop of funhouse glitz.

Dedication excerpts, July 6, 1957.

"I am very happy to be on this ground today because this town is called Independence and always when I hear Harry Truman referred to as 'the man from Independence,' I always want to add that he is a man of independence, courage, fidelity, devotion to duty and to the things that are best for his community, his state, his country, and the world." — Sam Rayburn

"It was during Mr. Truman's administration, with the experience of the second World War behind us, that an end was put to any possibility that the United States could ever return to a policy of isolation and self-sufficiency. Out of the conflict had come the discovery of nuclear fission with implications for future good or evil and posing a great challenge to the human family. Although we did not seek it, world-wide responsibility was thrust upon us." — Earl Warren

"There is great reason why the documentation of these special epochal periods in American history should not be concentrated in Washington. In recent years man's quest into the fundamental laws of nature has no doubt opened great vistas of benefit to mankind. But also man has not risen to the moral levels of their control for peace purposes, nor have governments been able to assure their control. The dispersal of the precious records of our history into local communities has greatly added to their safety." — Herbert Hoover

"Everyone familiar with the political scene of the past 10 years is well aware that Mr. Truman and I have not seen eye to eye — to put it mildly — on many things. You might even say that we have, in our political relationship, upheld the highest traditions of the Hatfields and

McCoys. But whatever our differences may have been in the past — and I doubt that there were any hatchets buried in that cornerstone this morning — there has never been, to my knowledge, anything of personal bitterness between us. Nor will there ever be, I am certain."
— Charles A. Halleck

Directions: From the North, take Interstates 29 or 35 south to Kansas City. Proceed east on Missouri Highway 24 to the corner of 24 and Delaware Street. Turn right there at the Truman Library. From the East, take Interstate 70 west. Go north on Noland Drive. Exit at Highway 24 west and go to the library. From the South, take Interstate 435 north. Exit east on Highway 24 and go to the library. From the West, take Interstate 35 east. Exit east on Highway 24 and proceed to the library.

The Truman Library — now, a.k.a. "The Truman" — at night. Said its namesake: "I had the job and I had to do it." Polls suggest that most Americans think he did it well. *(Truman Library)*

CHAPTER 7

OUR HOUSE

HUGH SIDEY GREW UP IN
Iowa, and writes lyrically about the banal
and giant, self-assured and unself-confi-
dent, shy and strutting people that is the
people of the United States.

"They come from different places,
with a common goal," he observed in
TIME in 1991. "They want to give birth
and grow and love and laugh and die,
bonded and sustained by the land, which
is the oldest way of life Americans know."

For more than two centuries, the
presidency has been America's reigning
way of leadership. Winston Churchill
once said, "An empty cab drove up and
Clement Attlee got out." Below, photos
from Eisenhower through Kennedy via
Johnson to Nixon show the libraries of
America's presidents at mid-20th Century. Visit any, or all. You will find few
empty cabs.

Dwight D. Eisenhower Library. Abilene, Kansas. *(Eisenhower Library)*

John Fitzgerald Kennedy Library. Boston, Massachusetts. *(Kennedy Library)*

Lyndon Baines Johnson Library and Museum. Austin, Texas. *(LBJ Library Collection)*

Richard Nixon Library and Birthplace. Yorba Linda, California. *(Nixon Library and Birthplace)*

CHAPTER 8

BELOVED IKE
DWIGHT D. EISENHOWER LIBRARY

(U.S. Navy)

THE FIRST PRESIDENT THAT I recall began the Peace Corps, spawned the Alliance for Progress, and composed "a picture of total urbanity," one writer said — "the first true reflection in the Presidency of America at the turn of the mid-century, a country of city dwellers long gone from Main Street."

Yet John F. Kennedy was not the president most cardinal to my childhood of the late 1950s. That was a man first inaugurated when I was one year old — the Sunflower Son named Ike.

It may be fair to call Dwight Eisenhower the most beloved man in American history. In March 1955, a Gallup Poll revealed that 60 percent of *Democrats* wanted him as their nominee. Said the man who, in reflection, was a superb and civilizing president:

Where it all began. Portrait of Ike's family on the front porch of their Abilene home. Left to right: Roy, Arthur, Earl, David, Jacob, Dwight, Milton, and Ida. *(Dwight D. Eisenhower Library)*

"Everybody ought to be happy every day. Play hard, have fun doing it, and despise wickedness."

Think of Ike — to biographer Steven Ambrose, "a great and good man" and president — as parable of an almost Edwardian age. He linked the St. Lawrence Seaway, Interstate Highway System, first civil rights bill since 1875, and eight years of 1.5 percent inflation and *nonpareil* unity — a decade that pollster George Gallup says more Americans would choose to relive than any of this century.

Later, even many critics converted to Ike's peace and prosperity. "Never," wrote Pulitzer Prize recipient Theodore H. White, "did the [day] shine fairer across a great Nation than it did in the age of Eisenhower." Washington turns to power like a heliotrope does the sun. Ike's miracle was to show how decency could light even the swarmy cave of politics.

I STILL RECOLLECT MY FIRST ACT of political theatre — Ike at the 1960 Republican Convention — his smile out ahead of him, like Jim Ryun lapping the field. Years later, I joined the White House staff as a presidential speechwriter. One day, Ike dwarfed a meeting in the Roosevelt Room, a mahogany chamber off the Oval Office, where George Bush talked of policy, language, and ghosts of presidents past.

I asked which predecessors he most

admired. Bush named Lincoln, who abolished slavery and saved the Union. Theodore Roosevelt, who was what Bush wished to be — a president who preserved lands and wildlife for unborn generations. Finally, the West Point graduate who became general of the Army, president of Columbia University, the first Supreme Commander of NATO, and 34th president.

"I always liked Ike," Bush began. In fact, he revered Eisenhower as a man, Chief of the Allied Expeditionary Force — at 20, pilot Bush was shot down in World War II — and what Andrew Jackson was to Truman, Truman to Ford, and JFK to Bill Clinton. The frame of reference for their presidential orb.

"Why?" I said. To my left stood a patchwork of flags — notably, the United States' and the presidential seal. Across the room was the Nobel Peace Prize that TR received in 1906.

"He was bi-partisan. He brought people together. It was Congress and the President on the same side. We've lost so much of that since then," Bush said, twirling glasses in his hands. "He got the country moving in one direction, representing our best values along the way."

BUSH HOPED TO GOVERN LIKE Ike in the 1950s — more as president than politician, his model a plaque which topped Eisenhower's desk: "gently in manner, strong in deed." I needed little goading, and soon speech references dubbed "beloved Ike" began sprouting like Kansas fireflies. Aides joked that the moniker was really Eisenhower's first name.

Finally, the word came forth from staff secretary Jim Cicconi, Bush's fellow Texan and assistant to the president — *no mas*. "If I see that phrase again," Cicconi said, tongue in cheek, "I think I'll go back and vote for [Adlai] Stevenson." Pity: Our research files bulged with beloved Ikeisms. I am sure the president never knew of this decree.

Dwight Eisenhower was not the kindly stick figure/father figure drawn by critics and admirers. Reserved, he was mercurial. His temper hovered, but was limited to intimates. Most people despair over the big things — separation, death, estrangement. Ike erupted at the mundane — a lousy 7-iron, a balky jeep ignition, the gnawing din of mid-Manhattan.

He could be cold. The journalist Hedley Donovan shocked peers by calling Ike smarter than Stevenson, but not as nice. Eisenhower used aides to deflect criticism. Richard Nixon wrote how General Walter Bedell Smith, Ike's World War II chief of staff, tearfully invoked his boss. "I was only Ike's prat boy. Ike always had to have a prat boy." His words may be true. Nixon's point is irrelevant.

Many leaders are loved in their own countries, or admired in others. Eisenhower was revered globally as the mirror of America. Hearing Bush, I remembered how Ike was adored in India and Italy, Budapest and Berlin. What was it that so set him apart?

FIRST, EISENHOWER WAS A MAN of exceeding good will — a healer, not hater, who believed America to be divinely blessed. "In politics," his vice president noted, "the natural reaction is to have strong hatreds one way or the other. Ike didn't fit that pattern. He didn't think of people who disagreed with him as being the enemy. He thought, 'They don't agree with me.'"

Ike's temperance was evident here and abroad. At home, he believed that "the road to success must be down the middle." Abroad, knowing war, he hated it — said Ike in 1955 to the Soviets, "I've had enough of war." So he launched the age of summitry, believing that "open skies" could open hearts. Three decades later, what Bush termed the Revolution of '89 evolved from the morality and humanity of a soldier, diplomat, and five-star general.

Eisenhower discusses the Suez crisis with Secretary of State John Foster Dulles in the fall of 1956. Ike forced Britain, France, and Israel to withdraw from Egypt. *(National Park Service)*

President and Mrs. Eisenhower host Premier and Mrs. Nikita Khrushchev on the latter's 1959 trip to the United States. Their smiles belie the Cold War at its height. *(U.S. Navy)*

Next, Ike encapsuled his age and place — almost *becoming* the American 1950s. He loved Zane Grey, Lawrence Welk, and TV westerns. As Bush told Eisenhower's Centenary Commission in 1990, Ike's favorite band was Fred Waring and the Pennsylvanians. (Sadly, the president axed the line, "Of course, his fox trot was better than mine. As Barbara says, 'Whose isn't?'")

Eisenhower played the great American sports — baseball and football — at West Point, and followed them as president. Many cannot watch the Army-Navy game without still conjuring its symbol. Ike's passion for the links became a na-

tional belly laugh. He built a putting green near the Oval Office and, like Arnold Palmer in the '50s, buoyed golf's appeal. (Out, too, went the Centenary sentence: "You'll know I've had a similar impact if the next few years produce a seniors' fishing tour." Bush could be sensitive about equating himself with Ike.)

It is true that Ike was not a linguist; to most Americans, that enhanced, not harmed, his honest sense of identity. "He was one of us — we trusted him to act on behalf of us," Bush told the commission. Then came a passage the president kept in. "In fact, fracturing syntax, Ike even spoke like us." Grin, and empathy.

"Come to think of it, now I know why he's among my favorite Presidents."

FINALLY, IKE WAS BELOVED BEcause of who he was — which, in turn, led America to trust what he did as president.

Kennedy, Johnson, Nixon, and Bush had splendid resumes when they ran for president. None included the words "preserved civilization." Eisenhower's did. Most leaders try to save the world after they get elected. Ike did it the other way around. He provided what he prescribed for democracy: "faith, love of freedom, intelligence, and energy." Eclipsing biography, he was as much a citizen of London as of Abilene.

On November 30, 1989, Bush went to the Mediterranean island of Malta for his first meeting with Soviet President Mikhail Gorbachev. A day later, he gave his only speech of the summit to 5,000 sailors on the USS *Forrestal*. My first draft ended with the prayer Franklin Roosevelt spoke, on D-Day, over nationwide radio. Instead, Bush asked for beloved Ike — and his remarks concluded so:

"Let me close with a moment you're too young to remember — but which wrote a glorious page in American history. It occurred on D-Day as Dwight Eisenhower addressed the sailors, soldiers, and airmen of the Allied Expeditionary Force.

"'You are about to embark,' he told them, 'upon a great crusade ... The eyes of the world are upon you. The hopes and prayers of liberty-loving people march with you.' Then, Ike spoke this moving prayer: 'Let us all beseech the blessing of Almighty God, upon this great and noble undertaking.'

"Like the men of D-Day, you, too, are the hope of 'liberty-loving people' everywhere. As the Navy has been in wartime — and in peacetime — keeping our hearts aflight — and our faith unyielding. Sacrificing time away from

The grin that transcended tongue, and time. Ike visits troops on the eve of D-Day. (*U.S. Army*)

your homes so that other Americans can sleep safely in theirs."

His voice wavering, the president observed, "Today, the walls of oppression are tumbling down because of what you have done to keep America's defenses up. God bless you and our 'great and noble undertaking.' And God bless the United States of America."

Listening, many recalled their parents, who rejoiced when Ike was elected in 1952, and their grandparents, who cried when he died on March 28, 1969, and their hometown, which supported him, and Ike's Kansas boyhood, which molded him, and of signposts from Fort Ord to Normandy to Guildhall to Arlington — and how nearing the year 2000, only FDR eclipses him in Henry Luce's American Century.

Once, after a fit of Eisenhower temper, his mother told the then-10-year-old, "He that conquereth his own soul is greater than he who taketh a city." He did, and enriched the nation's.

Beloved Ike, indeed.

★ ★ ★

Dwight D. Eisenhower Library. Daniel D. Holt, Director. Southeast Fourth Street, Abilene, Kansas 67410. Phone:

The placards spoke for America and the world. Ike campaigns in Baltimore in September 1952. He won by a landslide — the GOP's first presidential victory in 24 years. (*Maryland State Police*)

Dwight D. Eisenhower Library. Abilene, Kansas. Think of Ike's 1950s, the author writes, "as an almost Edwardian age … of peace and *nonpareil* unity." *(Eisenhower Library)*

(913) 263-4751. Fax: (913) 263-4218. Web site: http://history.cc.ukans.edu/ heritage/abilene/ikectr.html or http:// sunsite.unc.edu/lia/president/ eisenhower.html.

Visitors have included: Presidents Johnson, Nixon, Ford, and Reagan. First Ladies Lady Bird Johnson and Pat Nixon. Vice President Dan Quayle. General Colin Powell. Ambassador Vernon Walters. Cabinet Secretaries Herbert Brownell, Neil McElroy, William Rogers, and Fred Seaton. Senators Frank Carlson, Harry Darby, Robert Dole, and Nancy Kassebaum. Milton, John S. D., David, and Julie Eisenhower. Evangelist Billy Graham. Mrs. Bob (Delores) Hope. Actor Jerry Mathers. Historian Steven Ambrose. Writers Merle Miller and Richard Reeves.

Hours: Daily, 9 A.M. to 4:45 P.M. (The museum and Visitors Center are open until 5:45 P.M. Memorial Day to Labor Day.) Open every day, except New Year's Day, Thanksgiving, and Christmas. (Research facilities, Monday through Friday, 9 A.M. to 4:45 P.M. No fee, but advance written request must be made to the Director for Research). Admission: Children age 15 years and under, free to all buildings. Others, $2 to the exhibit areas of the museum. Free parking. Library gift shop is open during regular hours.

"AMERICA TODAY IS JUST AS strong as it needs to be," Dwight Eisenhower declaimed at his library dedication. "America is the strongest nation in the world and she will never be defeated or damaged seriously by anyone from the outside. Only Americans can ever hurt America." In Abilene, that thought seems as dim as the elegiac dark.

Unlike the typical library under a single roof, Ike's facility links five structures on a 22.5-acre park-like mall. The museum. The library. Eisenhower's boyhood home. A Visitors Center. The Place of Meditation. The pentagon of sites is named the Eisenhower Center.

Its roots date to fall 1944. Charles de Gaulle entered Paris. B-29s raided Japan from Saipan. Allied paratroopers dropped onto Germany like avenging angels. In New York, Albert T. Reid, a great artist and cartoonist, conceived an idea for his home state of Kansas — a museum to reunite veterans, etch the Great War via mural, and house Ike's and other vets' WW II souvenirs.

In early 1945, Reid contacted an Abilene newspaper editor, Charles Harger, who met local groups from the Lions to the Chamber of Commerce. They unanimously decided to proceed with a memorial. Reid pitched backers in New York, Chicago, and other cities. What set fundraising off was Ike's

The museum's World War II display features tanks, guns, parachutes, Ike's five-star auto, and other materiel from history's most grand and awful conflict. *(Eisenhower Library)*

June 20, 1945 return to Kansas. "The proudest thing I can say," he told the crowd, "is that I am from Abilene." The blizzard of handclapping presaged groundbreaking on April 21, 1952.

Two months later, Eisenhower announced for president in Abilene's city park. The museum opened April 3, 1954. That year, Ike signed the Presidential Libraries Act and chose Abilene for his library. *Its* groundbreaking was the day before Ike's birthday — October 13, 1959.

"I hope that [future generations]," he said, "as we today, are concerned primarily with the ideals, principles, and trends that provide guides to a free, rich, and peaceful future."

Those guides, as Ike might tell you, have still not found their way home.

IN 1962, THE FIRST NEGRO EN-rolled at the University of Mississippi, the Cuban Missile Crisis hinted Armageddon, and John Glenn became the first American to orbit the earth. The Eisenhower Library was dedicated May 1 — its exterior, Kansas limestone, and interior, imported marble. Its taste was closest to Ike's in the bronze work of buffalo heads and native bluestem grass.

"This library that you are dedicating

Eisenhower administration exhibits etch 1952's victorious "Whistle Stop" campaign tour — and other chapters of Ike's 1953-61 two-term daybook as president. *(Eisenhower Library)*

Each researcher admitted to the library works in this room. As at all presidential libraries, they receive the help and counsel of a trained archival staff. *(Eisenhower Library)*

today is a monument to a man, a man who is deeply beloved by all the American people," then-Vice President Lyndon Johnson said. It included a research room, archival stacks, and a photographic laboratory. Today, its 400 manuscript collections vaunt the papers and records of 15 cabinet secretaries, 55 presidential aides, and Eisenhower family members, including Mamie Doud, John S.D., and Milton Eisenhower.

The library holds more than 22 million pages. Of special interest are World War II and the 1950s-60s and their papers of 33 general officers, including Ike's chief of staff, General Bedell Smith. Daunting illusion are also more than 210,000 photos, 585,000 feet of motion picture film, and 2,300 hours of audio recordings.

The product is a prism and progenitor of Ike's life and the events of his military and civilian career. "Think of Ike like Roosevelt," said library director Daniel Holt. (How many libraries compare themselves to FDR's!) "Both were giants — FDR, a Navy man; Ike, Army. Neither was an intellectual, but both valued scholarship. Each library reflects them — Hyde Park, the patrician; Abilene, the small-town boy made good."

Dedicating the library, University of

Ike's boyhood home, restored to the time of his mother's death. Like most U.S. presidents, he enjoyed what he termed "the great and priceless privilege of being raised in a small town." *(Eisenhower Library)*

Kansas Chancellor W. Clarke Wescoe dubbed it "a beginning, a flowering of opportunity from the boy of Abilene to the boys and girls." It blossoms here in 24,000 books about Ike's life and age (1890-1969). Read, browse, see a film in the Visitors Center's 300-seat auditorium, and tour the property's other sites. All show America as a family affair, sure and certain of its place:

• Ike's home, typical of late-19th Century Kansas, was occupied by family members from 1898 through 1946. When his mother died, her five sons gave it to the Eisenhower Foundation. The two-story interior — same color, books,

and furniture — is restored to the 1940s time of Ida Eisenhower's death.

Explore the piano on which all five boys took lessons; Ike's bedroom, which he shared with a brother; and sofa handmade by his great-grandfather, an 1880s professional weaver. Ida's potted plants in the bay window of the front parlor still bloom like Operation Overlord did under Ike.

• In 1966, the center opened its Place of Meditation. When Eisenhower died, he was buried with his first-born son, Doud Dwight, who died at age three of scarlett fever, and later Mamie. The chapel mixes stained glass, walnut

Five years after Ike left office, the Eisenhower Presidential Library Commission completed this chapel. *(Eisenhower Library)*

IN A JUNE 1945 CEREMONY HELD in the ancient Guildhall, Eisenhower was made a "Freeman of the City of London." After his first day as president, Ike told his diary that "today just seems like a continuation of all I've been doing since July '41." The museum bares the churnings of what Ike was, and did, through more than 35,000 objects, of which one-third are on display at a time.

Like America, the museum hero-worships World War II. Ike's orders, awards, and medals given during and after the war head its holdings. Too, photo, document, and *objets d'art*: Ike's hand-written D-Day note, "In case of failure," dated June 5, 1944; the "Eisenhower jacket" modeled after the British battle jacket; Ike's chair from the D-Day Planning Table used at Stanwell House, London; Eisenhower's Philippine duty and his original pilot's license and wings; and exhibit on the Nazis' May 7, 1945 unconditional surrender.

Stroll Military Hall, and see Ike's 1942 Cadillac staff car, model of the artificial harbor — Mulberry — D-Day keep-sakes, and Bedell Smith's shield case with ribbons from foreign governments. Turn a corner to the "White House Years" Ike portrait by Thomas E. Stephens, drafts of his 1953 inaugural address, and gifts like the Frederick Remington "Bronco Buster" and two Charles Russell bronzes of Indians.

woodwork, travertine marble walls, and crochet stitching Ike's handwritten first inaugural address prayer. Nearby lies a Georgia granite statue of Ike given by Kansas Senator Harry Darby, and graced by quotes and insignia from Ike's life of handshakes and hurrahs.

• The museum, dedicated Veterans Day 1954. Today's exhibition space — more than 30,000 square feet — doubles the original building's. Its galleries include: "Introductory," Eisenhower's life; "Military," Ike's career in khaki; "Presidential," the trends and events of the 1950s; "First Lady," Mamie as mother, war wife, volunteer, and role model; and "Changing," traveling exhibitions as the orb of evolution.

In the '50s, Americans sang, "Once in love with Mamie." From hair to attire, Mrs. Eisenhower's exhibit shows how Ike's wife affected her place and age. *(Eisenhower Library)*

Was 1950s America more soft and settled? "Take a look at Mrs. Eisenhower's nearby exhibit," laughed Holt, "and you've got the answer." Enjoy her White House china, first inaugural suit, and doll collection fashioned after the Smithsonian Institution's First Lady gowns. Plumb the museum's political cartoon collection, and array of campaign buttons, jewelry, and posters. Judge Eisenhower's paintings — "it relaxed me," he said — and other portraits, landscapes, and American primitives.

"Eisenhower has, and retains, a magic in American politics that is peculiarly his," wrote Theodore White. "He

makes people happy." Proof drapes photos of Ike in Abilene — with friends fishing in 1907 along the Smokey Hill River; 1953's wave from an open car during Abilene's "Welcome Mr. President" parade; opening the 1954 wing of the Eisenhower Museum; and 1962's portrait of the Eisenhower family on the front porch of their home.

By now, even Democrats can be heard rhyming, "I Like Ike."

"FROM THE TIME OF KING SOLOmon," Kansas Governor John Anderson observed in 1962, "men everywhere have taken pride in fine buildings and fine architecture, and now in Kansas, we have such a structure." The permanent structure is lush with temporary exhibits.

In 1990, Eisenhower centennial events included a conference on '50s civil rights — symposium on the "Living White House," with children and grandchildren of recent presidents — and USO bash, World War II aircraft show, and Billy Graham service on the anniversary of Ike's birth.

In 1994, on D-Day at 50, the library hosted a conference of military scholars as well as British, American, French, and German veterans. A year later, Ike's 1945 return to Abilene was hailed by a parade and seminar which studied, among other things, how Ike did his job. Sessions included a Mamie tribute — "Pretty in Pink or Iron Lady" — and "Debunking Eisenhower Myths." Yes, he had a temper. No, Ike did not follow UFOs.

James Fenimore Cooper wrote a novel, *Satanstoe*, about Everyman ruling his own terrain — his idyllic habitat — without impingement, free. Did such a place exist? It seems so at this site. "I come from the very heart of America," said Ike. Freighted with memory, the Eisenhower Library shows a First Citizen of the Globe.

Half-a-century after World War II, the Eisenhower Library introduced a temporary display showing where, and how, U.S. troops helped win the Cold War. *(Eisenhower Library)*

★ ★ Windows on the White House ★ ★

★ ★ ★

Dedication excerpts, May 1, 1962.

"Seventy-two years ago, during a brief sojourn in Texas, a child was born to a son of this Abilene family, and less than a year later, still a babe in arms, he was returned to this spot to spend his formative years ... It may be odd, but not [in]significant, that a great museum should grow where a boy planted potatoes, a great library, where he planted sweet corn." — University of Kansas Chancellor W. Clarke Wescoe

"When we see movies and the stage, and books and periodicals, using vulgarity, sensuality — indeed, downright filth — to sell their wares, do you think that America has advanced morally as we have materially? When we see our very art forms so changed that we seem to have forgotten the works of Michelangelo and Leonardo da Vinci, and speak in the press in terms of a piece of canvas that looks like a broken down tin lizzie, loaded down with paint, has been driven over, is this improvement? What has happened to our concept of beauty and decency and morality?" — Dwight D. Eisenhower

"One day ... in the heat of the campaign of '52, when the Speaker [Sam Rayburn] was talking about the glories of the Democratic Party, some fellow way back in the back that thought he just had to vote for President Eisenhower — even though he had voted the Democratic ticket all of his life — spoke up and said, 'Mr. Speaker, wasn't General Eisenhower born in your own old [Texas'] Fourth District?' And he knew that the Speaker had never found anybody that had been born there that he could find anything wrong with. And that had him! And the Speaker ran his hand over his bald head and said, 'Yes, and he was a mighty good baby!'"* — Lyndon B. Johnson

"As I stand here, my mind goes back to something that Senator [Harry] Darby just said. He recalled that this is the one-hundredth anniversary of my mother's birth. For those of the Eisenhower family, this statement has a very deep meaning ... because I think that all of her sons — indeed, all of her close relatives — would, today, like to think that she knows that they still revere her teachings, her strength, her refusal ever to admit defeat in small or great things. She was truly a remarkable person!" — Dwight Eisenhower

★ ★ ★

Directions: From the North, take Kansas Highway 15 (Buckeye Avenue) into

Ike and Mamie. Forget Ward and June Cleaver, or Lucy and Ricky Ricardo. To Middle America, they were the Nation's First Couple — in the 1950s, and now. *(Eisenhower Library)*

Abilene. Stay on 15 and turn left at the Eisenhower Library. From the East, take Interstate 70 west. Take the Abilene exit south on Highway 15 to the library. From the South, take Interstate 35 north past Wichita. Exit north on Highway 15 and proceed to the library. From the West, take I-70 east. Take the Abilene exit south on Highway 15 to the Eisenhower Library.

A man of peace, Ike helped win mankind's greatest war. This statue was dedicated in June 1985 near the Place of Meditation chapel. *(Eisenhower Library)*

Chapter 9

The Irish Brahmin
John Fitzgerald Kennedy Library

(John F. Kennedy Library)

He had brown hair, a perpetual tan, and a twist to his bite. By reputation, he put forth irony, a fluent phrase, and a graceful front when under pressure. Emphatic and sensitive by nature, he was not a hater, and sought endlessly to grasp other points of view. Expert at social intercourse, he was always ready with the hospitable word and beguiling gesture.

"The country is most barbarously large and final," William Bammer wrote in *The Gay Place*. "It is too much country ... spectral and remote. It is so wrongfully muddled and various that it is difficult to conceive of it all as a piece." John Fitzgerald Kennedy — Harvard '40, war hero, Pulitzer-winning author, U. S. Senate 1953-61, 35th president 1961-63 — was a piece then and now. Was he "large and final?" Is New York City, for all its bombast, a phantasmagoric place?

Born May 29, 1917 in the Boston suburb of Brookline, Kennedy synthesized the Gaelic mix of promise and foreboding. He learned history from his

President and Mrs. Kennedy — to William Styron, "creatures beyond legend" — with children
Caroline and John at the family compound in Hyannis Port in August 1962. *(Kennedy Library)*

mother, and politics from his father. He saw humor everywhere — in life's absurdities, improbabilities, and preposterous cant.

The Kennedy family had settled in Massachusetts only a century earlier. Joseph P. Kennedy, Jr., gave Jack a leg up and clear aim — win — from 1946's first House race through 1960's run for president. Money is said to be the mother's milk of politics. Kennedy's $200 million

pasteurized JFK's career. It did not spawn his son's detached, lyric style. "Jack," said Massachusetts Governor Paul Dever, "is the first Irish Brahmin."

Kennedy looked almost Arthurian — yet suffered from Addison's disease, an adrenal disorder then often fatal, and almost died in 1954. He touted "vig-ah," and preached the active — i.e. fast-lane — life, yet was a biographer and voracious reader. Rivals said that Papa Joe made him president. Was there a more-his-own man president than John F. Kennedy?

Shy, JFK chose politics' rock/sock-'em maelstrom. He was from, not of, it. In the 1960 Wisconsin Primary, a drunk tossed a glass in his face. Kennedy picked it up and said, "Here's your drink." His style gripped reporters. "History chooses to look past details of policies and personal peccadilloes," *Esquire* wrote two decades after Dallas. "Instead, it continues to shine on Kennedy's knighthood, his gallantry."

The Irish Brahmin made life a sudden magic place, but was no Boswell of the human condition. Such amalgams are hard to find.

JFK'S BLOOMED IN THE EARLY 1960s which hailed polarity, not uniformity, and how the presidency changed: from Main Street to New Frontier; businessmen to academics, unionists, and civil righters; a Protestant-only post to an equal-opportunity office. Pols once equated success with legislation. That changed with JFK. Most believe that chic wrote the prose of the legend that was Camelot.

In shorthand code, those disdaining Ike's 1950s regarded the early '60s as an epoch which reawakened the senses. America before Kennedy, they said, had been hypocritical and puritanical, som-

nolent, inhibited. As a young, Presbyterian, and *shabby-genteel* boy, on the other hand, my people thought the Age of Eisenhower possessed of a kindness that, in retrospect, seems virginal.

Only later, in a time when perspective was in season, did you see the working agreement which bound both then-rival camps. Their pillar was the keeper of the faith, defender of the peace, guardian of West Berlin, and scourge of "Godless Communism." Tom Wicker has termed Kennedy "the most fascinating might-have-been in American history." As a not-yet teenager, I sensed in his Era of Good Feeling a leader who already was.

What was myth, truth, and afterclap of Kennedy's 34 months as president? It is difficult to tell. The fact is that he almost never made it. To this day no one knows who was really elected in 1960. Fraud warped the outcome; Richard Nixon conjured a recount. Kennedy's edge flowed from rhetoric, political reflex, voting booths in Illinois and Texas, and TV presence.

As of 1960, no Catholic had been elected president. None had been a serious candidate since 1928. "I refuse to believe that I was denied the right to be president on the day I was baptized," he said in the West Virginia Primary. Brilliant! Protestants could show tolerance only by backing JFK. Astute, Kennedy could be as hard as Ike. He barbed of Nixon, "He went out the way he came in — no class." Hubert Humphrey later wrote that he had trouble forgetting the Kennedys' win-at-all-cost creed.

JFK's prose glossed a more poetic side. "Mr. Nixon and I, and the Republican and Democratic parties, are not suddenly frozen in ice or collected in amber since the two conventions," he said in 1960. "We are like two rivers which flow back through history, and you can judge the force, the power, and the direction of the rivers by studying where they rose and where they ran throughout their long course."

Before September, Nixon's river had cut deeper through America. Enter the medium that, Kennedy said, "more than anything, turned the tide." In 1950, we chitchatted around the radio. A decade later, 88 percent of families owned a television. A champion debater, Nixon accepted Kennedy's gauntlet of four TV tussles. The first, before 70 million viewers, turned expectation on its head. Nixon was sweaty, whiskered, and slack from illness. He addressed himself to Kennedy, like a pre-TV debater. Exuding charm, Kennedy addressed the camera.

Radio polls favored Nixon. Kennedy took the kinetic tube — and the election by less than 113,000 votes.

MIDWIVED BY TELEVISION, KENnedy christened it as president. He staged

Kennedy, with Soviet Premier Nikita Khrushchev, at the acidic 1961 Vienna summit. Khrushchev bullied the young U.S. president. Said JFK: "It's going to be a cold winter." *(Kennedy Library)*

America's Royal Couple, 1961-63. What was style, and substance? Both were capable of what F. Scott Fitzgerald called "an unbroken series of perfect gestures." *(Kennedy Library)*

interviews with network correspondents, flew foreign footage back for nightly news, and let cameras into the Oval Office. JFK was the first to stage live TV press conferences. Flaunting cool and humor, he soon owned the biggest show in town.

Ike and Mamie read Louis L'Amour, and liked TV dinners. The new First Family seemed to inhabit another orb. Kennedy's inaugural presaged change. "The Star Spangled Banner" was sung by black Marian Anderson. Robert Frost prepared a preface to his poem, "The

Gift Outright." Kennedy outshone each: "Let the word go forth from this time and place, to friend and foe alike, that the torch has been passed to a new generation of Americans." Suddenly, to paraphrase Ring Lardner, mediocrity seemed to be a side dish America had not ordered.

"Kennedy differed from any predecessor," a reporter wrote. "He was removed from the log cabin, and became president as America left the small town behind." His rapture misread the nation — since Kennedy, the Oval Office has oozed small-town America — but not the 35th president. JFK and Jackie cheered Pablo Casals, and invited Stravinsky, Isaac Stern, a ballet troupe, and Shakespeare company to perform. A group of Nobel Prize laureates became "the most extraordinary collection of talent…that has ever been gathered together at the White House — with the possible exception of when Thomas Jefferson dined alone."

Little in the Kennedy White House ran counter to self-congratulation. Writers, musicians, artisans, and academics lavished praise on the Irish Brahmin — and saw an idealized image of themselves. Yet all fact was not ennobling: JFK made a mess of the Bay of Pigs. On April 17, 1961, he withheld air cover from an anti-Castro, exile-led attack on Communist forces on Cuba's southern coast. It failed. Emboldened, Nikita Khrushchev thought him a bungler and provocateur. He bullied JFK at the

President Kennedy signing the Equal Pay Act. Such legislative triumphs occurred despite a coalition of Republicans and conservative Democrats on Capitol Hill. *(Kennedy Library)*

Nowhere was Kennedy's vow to "get America moving again" more fervid than the military. Here JFK visits U.S. troops at Fort Bragg, North Carolina, in October 1961. *(U.S. Army Signal Corp.)*

Vienna summit, built a wall to seal off West Berlin, and smirked when Kennedy pledged "before this decade is out" to land a man on the moon.

JFK abhorred losing. Once, he advertently upset the board while losing a game to old friend and Navy Undersecretary "Red" Fay. "One of those unfortunate incidents of life, Redhead," he said. "We'll never really know if the undersecretary was going to outmaneu-

ver the Commander in Chief." We do know landmarks from Kennedy's 1,010 days. Among them: He beat Khrushchev to the moon, and in a turning point on earth.

In fall 1962, the Soviets placed offensive missiles in Cuba. Slowly, Kennedy saw from aerial photos that Soviet launching pads were being built for intermediate long-range missiles. The pragmatist brooded. Should he strike by air?

To Kennedy, excellence meant the pursuit of one's powers. Before the 1962 baseball All-Star Game in Washington, he practiced throwing out the first ball in the Rose Garden. *(Kennedy Library)*

Trade Cuban missile bases for obsolete American missile bases in Turkey? JFK chose to "quarantine" shipments of military equipment to Cuba, and tell Khrushchev that nuclear attack from Cuba would mean "full retaliatory response upon the Soviet Union."

The Russians blinked, removing weapons. For a time the Cold War thawed. To the Peace Corps and Alliance for Progress add JFK's nuclear test-ban treaty. In 1960, he said, "I think it's time that America started moving again." In late 1963, Kennedy's sight moved toward re-election. Already in the bank

were a huge tax cut, steady growth, and low inflation. JFK now asked for deposits from aid to education to legislation against segregation. Congress refused. He needed a landslide — so, Texas — to turn popularity to muscle on Capitol Hill.

BY FALL 1963, KENNEDY'S PERsona linked a combination of images. His World War II boat, PT-109. His book, *Profiles in Courage*. Hatless, coatless health. An accent made-for-mimicry. A rocking chair to ease back pain. Sailing off the Cape, and touch football at Hyannis Port. A clan large enough to man both teams. Son John-John. Daughter Caroline, entering the West Lobby in her mother's high heels. Reporters asked about her father. "Oh," she said, "he's upstairs with his shoes and socks off, not doing anything." Jackie's elegance. Wrote *TIME*: "Hollywood would not have cast such a dazzling pair."

Other images soon rivaled the waves atop Excalibur. The Texas School Book Depository. Crumpled roses in the back seat of the president's limousine outside Parkland Hospital. Dried blood on Mrs. Kennedy's suit. The swearing-in of Lyndon Johnson with the widow at his side. Where were you on November 22? Part of us still is there. Enduring is a muddle of nightmare memory. Lee Oswald. Jack Ruby. John-John saluting. The riderless steed. The caisson's trek across the Potomac. Arlington Cemetery. Once, JFK had told a friend, "I could stay here forever."

"What remains as the loss ... is a certain feeling of possiblity," said *Le Figaro* of Paris, "of an elan, and — why not say it? — of an impression of beauty. These are not political qualities, but surely they

This 1946 photo etches Kennedy's grace. That year, he began his political career by winning a House seat. Ultimately, he brought romance and verve to America's Ship of State. *(Kennedy Library)*

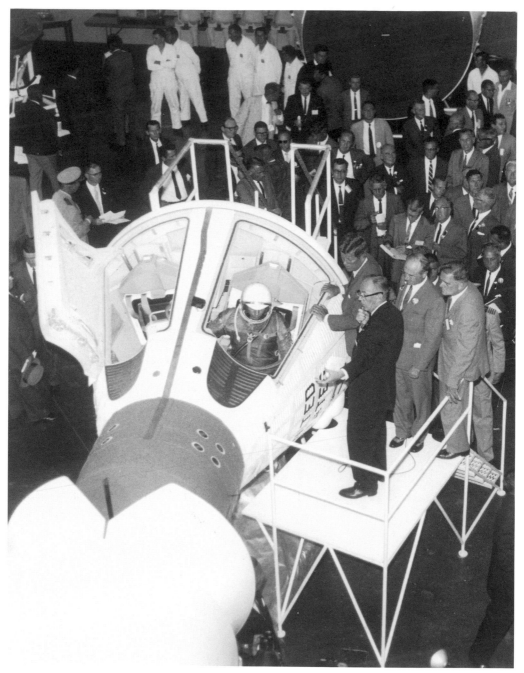

Why go to the moon? Kennedy said: "It is there." Nothing caught the New Frontier like the U.S. space program. Here JFK views a Gemini capsule in September 1962. *(Kennedy Library)*

John F. Kennedy Library. Boston, Massachusetts. Said the 35th president: "We all breathe the same air. We all cherish our children's future. And we are all mortal." *(Kennedy Library)*

are enduring legendary and mythological qualities."

Was Kennedy's the presidency in its Heaven — and/or America as Athens in the sky? Does it matter? Man requires a time to return to. For millions, JFK's America — dreamboat home, or age of remembered innocence — endures, lush and humming, as a place where one can leave the world alone.

★ ★ ★

John Fitzgerald Kennedy Library. Bradley Gerratt, Director. Columbia Point, Boston, Massachusetts 02125. Phone: (617) 929-4500. Fax: (617) 929-4538. Web site: http://www.cs.umb.edu/jfk library/index.htm.

Visitors have included: Presidents Carter and Clinton. First Ladies Lady Bird Johnson, Rosalynn Carter, and Hillary Clinton. Queen Sofia of Spain. Baseball player Joe DiMaggio. Actresses Lauren Bacall and Shirley MacLaine. Actor Arnold Schwarzenegger. Singers Harry Belafonte, Paul Simon, and Stevie Wonder. Broadcasters Tom Brokaw, Walter Cronkite, Bryant Gumbel, and Jane Pauley. Journalist Bob Woodward.

Congress erupted in applause when in 1961 JFK announced his design for outer space. In the space exhibit, listen to Kennedy describe America's destiny — here, and there. *(Kennedy Library)*

Hours: Daily, 9 A.M. to 5 P.M. Open every day, except New Year's Day, Thanksgiving, and Christmas. Admission: Children under age 6 free. Age 6 to 15, $2. Seniors over 62 and students with identification, $4. Others, $6. Group tours are urged in advance of trip to call (617) 929-4523. Free parking. Library gift shop is open during regular hours.

THE JOHN FITZGERALD KENNEDY

Library was dedicated on October 20, 1979. A sun-splashed day, the breeze off Cape Cod, and music from the Boston Symphony Orchestra washed 10,000 invited guests and other onlookers in boats on Dorchester Bay. "He loved this city with a patriot's love," said brother Senator Edward (Ted) Kennedy, or "Eddie," as JFK called him. "He loved the sea with a sailor's love. And so would have loved this site and the library his family and friends and country have built to celebrate his life."

On behalf of the family and the John F. Kennedy Library Corporation, Kennedy presented the library to America and heard JFK's children quote an English poem to "capture the spirit of our father." Stephen Spender's "I Think Continually of Those" ends: "Born of the sun they travelled a short while towards the sun, And left the vivid air signed with their honour."

Thirty-six million people contributed to the sixth presidential library operated by the National Archives. About 200,000 visitors and schoolchildren annually visit at Columbia Point on a 9.5-acre peninsula park of pine trees, wild roses, slopes of dune grass, and lawns along the water redolent of the Cape, where Kennedy spent his summers. It lies adjacent to the University of Massachusetts, four miles from downtown Boston, and is accessible by boat. JFK's 26-foot sloop, *Victura*, overlooks the entrance to Boston Harbor. Acquired by the Kennedys in 1930, the boat is named for a Greek word — its meaning, "bound to win."

"As a young man, Kennedy sailed *Victura* for fun and in races around the Cape," said library director Bradley Gerratt. "It's just one of the things here that bespeaks Kennedy's love of the water." Others are the harbor, offshore islands, Atlantic Ocean and the building. Its intersecting geometric forms, de-

The Second World War shaped and defined JFK. (His Navy uniform, above.) "I don't remember the Depression," he told one writer. "Ask me about the war." *(Kennedy Library)*

signed by I.M. Pei, and surfaces of concrete and glass evoke a sense of feel and place.

Forever — The Young Man and the Sea.

THE HEART OF KENNEDY'S 135,000-square foot complex is a nine-story white precast concrete tower, 125 feet high, which abuts a glass-enclosed pavilion. It contains an office, research,

The miracle is not that Kennedy barely won the 1960 Election. The wonder is that he won, at all. From Stevenson via Johnson to JFK, relive the greatest campaign of our time. *(Kennedy Library)*

and document storage facilities, two 230-seat theatres, and an 18,000-square foot exhibition area. Collections about Kennedy and mid-20th Century American government tug at your chest — 32 million pages of documents, 180,000 photographs, seven million feet of film, and 5,000 hours of sound recordings. "We celebrate the past," JFK tells you, "to awaken the future."

Kennedy's papers exceed 8.4 million pages. They are divided into: personal (1917-1963), especially manuscripts for his books, *Why England Slept*

and *Profiles in Courage*; pre-presidential (1947-1961), JFK's 14-year career as congressman and senator; and presidential (1961-1963), notably office files as kept by personal secretary Evelyn Lincoln. Other lights include the papers of Robert F. and Edward Kennedy and photos of RFK, Rose Kennedy's of the Kennedy and Fitzgerald families, and Ernest Hemingway. Note the original drafts of the Nobel Prize-winning author, including *A Farewell to Arms* and *For Whom the Bell Tolls*.

"To some, papers are dry sawbones,"

said Gerratt. "We think of them as flesh and blood." Arresting are Kennedy's public speeches and press conferences, and meetings he taped secretly in 1962-63. Newly released tapes show JFK's fear that 1962's Cuban Missile Crisis might provoke nuclear war. They include a CIA briefing on the Soviet military presence, review of the president's decision to order a naval quarantine, and critique by congressional leaders who wanted him to declare an act of war.

In October 1962, Churchill's "Terrible Ifs" seemed ready to cause mankind's horrific end. Instead, JFK's blockade worked. Yet many under age, say, 40, cannot even recall a Kennedy administration. The original museum relied on memory. Its effect waned as demographics grayed. "More of our visitors weren't alive in 1963," said Gerratt. "So we figured, 'Let's reintroduce JFK to them.' We wanted to provide a sort of 'you are there' sense of immediacy."

On October 29, 1993, President Clinton rededicated the library's new interior. Its armament — Kennedy's own words, *sans* interpretation or analysis. "[We wanted] to have President Kennedy convey," said daughter Caroline, "[what] he represented to a world confronting a dangerous time." JFK speaks in three New Museum theaters and 20 exhibit videos. Background objects are as eclectic as the sailor/ Ivy Leaguer/ touch football player/ Pulitzer recipient — here, a ship model from Nikita Khrushchev; there, JFK's Oval Office rocking chair.

Camelot starts with a *precis* of Kennedy's life and leads to a film of his roots — immigrant, and political. Narrated by JFK, the 17-minute movie traces his education, South Pacific war service, time in Congress, and victory at the 1960 Los Angeles Democratic Convention. "Then, enter the time where JFK became America's," said Gerratt. The years of rise are ineluctable.

Walk through the re-created Los Angeles Sports Arena, where JFK was nominated for president. Pass a stylized "Main Street, USA, 1960." Visit a storefront campaign headquarters. In an appliance and variety store, a TV set plays commercials and programs of the time. Then, via video, join Kennedy and his opponent, Vice President Richard Nixon, in a campaign with fire in its blood. A replica, including the original soundboard, of the Chicago WBBM-TV studio, invokes the first presidential debate. On Election Night, CBS and NBC paint what Jackie later called "the longest night in history."

The exhibit ends with the candidate now president-elect.

"HE AND I HAD A SPECIAL BOND," Ted Kennedy said of Jack, "despite the

14 years between us. He taught me to ride a bicycle, throw a forward pass, and sail against the wind." On January 20, 1961, Kennedy's bond adjoined America's. In an open theatre, watch his swearing-in and hear the inaugural address.

Next, pass via a symbolic portal — JFK is now president — to a long corridor with marble floor, red carpeting, and woodwork like the White House. Rooms off the corridor house exhibits from the Peace Corps to manned space program. Meet aides and cabinet officials — JFK's "ministry of talent" — and move to the International Affairs exhibit. It links, among other things, Food for Peace, the Alliance for Progress, access to West Berlin, and the cloud of Laos and Viet Nam.

A video stars Kennedy at televised press conferences. A few steps lead to a 70-seat theatre — and period footage of a 20-minute film retrieving 1962's Thirteen Days of Crisis. Also: film of the countdown and launch of Alan Shepard's spacecraft; Kennedy's memos to NASA personnel; models of early manned spacecraft; film of the president visiting Cape Canaveral; and a replica of John Glenn's space suit.

Enter a room to see a copy of the Limited Nuclear Test Ban Treaty and excerpts from Kennedy's speeches on peace and disarmament. Once, he told

writer William Manchester, "It doesn't really matter as you and I are concerned. What really matters is the children." JFK's played in the Oval Office — recreated as it looked during his 1963 TV address on civil rights. Keepsakes include a copy of his desk — for original, see Clinton's Oval Office — JFK's globe of the world in 1961, and ship models, scrimshaw, and other vestments of the sea.

"I do not think it altogether inappropriate to introduce myself to this audience," Kennedy told a press luncheon at the end of a 1961 trip to France. "I am the man who accompanied Jacqueline Kennedy to Paris, and I have enjoyed it." Recapture artists in the East Room, Jackie's trademark pillbox hat, and Emmy Award she got for her 1962 CBS-TV White House tour. You will feel like JFK upon seeing her at Paris' first evening event: "Well," he said at last, "I'm dazzled."

Visit a re-created residency. Sample family photos, editorial cartoons, and video of Kennedy's state visit home to Ireland in 1963. Then, leave the White House, enter a dark corridor, and relive Kennedy's death through broadcaster Walter Cronkite's bulletin. Monitors recall November 22, and the funeral. The corridor widens to a circular plot, lit only by nine transparencies. They mark places around the world named after JFK.

The library greets a visitor with artifacts from The Thousand Days. A re-created Oval Office features JFK's desk, rocking chair, and model of the USS *Constitution*. *(Kennedy Library)*

TO WHAT AVAIL? THE NEARBY "Legacy Room" hints reply. It uses interactive computers to judge Kennedy's influence, and lets you sift through books, photo albums, video, and objects in drawers and exhibit cases. The display banners JFK as pioneer. A section of the Berlin Wall, donated by the German government, recalls "*Ich bin ein Berliner.*" Clinton tells how, attending Boy's Nation in 1963, he met him at the White House.

Leaving, a visitor samples a 110-foot-high glass pavilion, 45-foot by 26-foot United States flag, and the annual Profile in Courage Award, given to an individual of political courage as Kennedy explained it in his book. Library photos lend further definition. One shows JFK leaning over his desk. The text reads: "Communism. Nuclear War. The Struggle for Civil Rights. No wonder his back hurt." In another, he looks skyward through binoculars: "John Kennedy wasn't the first politician to promise his constituents the moon. But he was the first to deliver it."

You look up and to the left, and see again the boat — *Victura* — that Kennedy sailed from its 1930 launch through

November 1963 — and from there to the melange of ocean, sky, and city. Then, on a wall this quotation from John F. Kennedy's inaugural address: "All this will not be finished in the first one hundred days, nor will it be finished in the life of this administration, nor even perhaps in our lifetime on this planet. But let us begin."

Dedication excerpts, October 20, 1979.

"I can see him now, standing by the shore, feeling the salt breeze, drinking in the beauty of this harbor, recalling its rich history and the great events that took place here when America was born. He would look out across the ocean to the horizon and beyond. Peering through the mists of time, he would see

Greeting Peace Corps volunteers in the Rose Garden. "You are serving your country," JFK told them, not focusing on money and a career. "We owe you a debt of gratitude." *(Kennedy Library)*

his immigrant heritage, the green and rocky shores of the land of his ancestors, the Ireland whence he came." — Edward Kennedy

"On that November day almost 16 years ago, a terrible moment was frozen in the lives of many of us here. I remember that I had climbed down from the seat of a tractor, unhooked a farm trailer and walked into my warehouse to weigh a load of grain. I was told by a group of farmers that the President had been shot. I went outside, knelt on the steps and began to pray. In a few minutes, I learned that he had not lived. It was a grievous personal loss. My President. I wept openly, for the first time in more than 10 years, for the first time since the day that my own father died." — Jimmy Carter

"It was all so brief. The thousand days are like an evening gone. But they are not forgotten. Those whose lives he touched will never be the same. They responded to his call, devoting their own lives to his country and bringing out the best in others as he brought out the best in them." — Edward Kennedy

"At the time, the tragedy in Dallas seemed an isolated convulsion of madness. But in retrospect, it appears near the beginning of a time of darkness. From Viet Nam to Cambodia, from Los

The night before he died, Kennedy talked of old men with dreams and young men with vision. To millions, he combined both. *(Kennedy Library)*

Angeles to Memphis, from Kent State to Watergate, the American spirit suffered under one shock after another, and the confidence of our people was deeply shaken." — Jimmy Carter

Directions: From the South, take Route 3/Interstate 93 (Southeast Expressway) to Dorchester. Take Exit 14 to Morrissey Boulevard. Follow signs to the University of Massachusetts and the JFK Library. From the North, take Route I-93 or Rte. 1/I-95 south to Boston and onto the S.E. Expressway (Rte. 3/I-93). Take Exit 15, and follow signs. From the West, take the Massachusetts Turnpike (Route I-90) to "Expressway South" (Rte. 3/I-93) and southbound to Exit 15. Follow signs to UMass and the JFK Library.

CHAPTER 10

COLOSSUS
LYNDON BAINES JOHNSON
LIBRARY AND MUSEUM

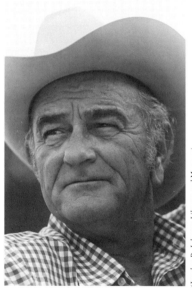

NAPOLEON SAID, "ABILITY IS fine, but give me commanders who have luck." America's 36th president fused instinct, empathy, intellect, and a raw feel for power — everything but chance. Luck was the avenging angel of Lyndon Johnson's administration.

LBJ followed John Kennedy as a MediaAge Leader — a wheeler-dealer in a time of Image TV. Hot, he hoped to seem cool. Uncut, he paraded the propriety he thought people wanted. He sought favor, craved consensus, and often befuzzed his position. As president, his persona seemed at odds with the man.

Special assistant Jack Valenti wrote

that Johnson was "a classic Achilles figure, immensely human, often commanding in presence, and noble in aim. Both were flawed by human error and a misperception of ultimate reality in a war seemingly without end." The war — Viet Nam — ended his presidency. It should not dim the memory of America's Falstaff in the Saddle.

Once, Johnson parodied an introduction that even he thought immodest. "I wish my parents were alive to hear those words. My father would have enjoyed them. And my mother would have believed them." Aides enjoyed telling stories they knew might seem unbelievable. Fact or pose — who could tell with LBJ? Why wouldn't he force J. Edgar Hoover to retire? "I'd rather have him inside the tent pissing out than outside pissing in."

To grasp Johnson meant knowing Texas — its beauty of peach orchards and berry fields and streams, falling away in endless sequence — and everywhere a sense of impatience with limits of any kind. Here LBJ heard train whistles that spoke of infinite possibility — "child's dreams," John Connally said in a 1973 eulogy to his mentor and benefactor, "[that] could be as wide as the sky and his future as green as winter oats because this, after all, was America."

Ahead was a Gulliver life and Lilliputian end. A friend observed, "He was clawed to death by lesser men."

A Lone Star power couple: Congressman Lyndon and Lady Bird Johnson flank the '30s United States Capitol. (*Johnson family photo*)

THERE WAS NOTHING PEE-WEE about Johnson's becoming president. He looked born-for, and larger-than, the office — Paul Bunyan straight out of Johnny Appleseed by way of Pecos Bill.

"Mr. Speaker, Mr. President ... my fellow Americans," he told Congress on

November 27, 1963, five days after being sworn in, "all I have I would have given gladly not to be standing here today." Kennedy had said, "Let us begin." Johnson urged, "Today, in this moment of new resolve ... let us continue." LBJ often likened Franklin Roosevelt to his daddy. The son now began a determined stab to match FDR's abiding will.

In early 1964, LBJ signed bills to aid college construction, wilderness areas, and urban mass transportation. Also passed: Kennedy's $11.5 billion tax cut, the Economic Opportunity Act, and Head Start, Neighborhood Youth Corps, Job Corps, and VISTA. In his first address to Congress, Johnson said, "We have talked long enough in this country about equal rights. We have talked for one hundred years or more. It is time to write the next chapter, and to write it in the book of law." Congress did, passing a civil rights bill that desegregated public facilities.

What Kennedy had proposed, Johnson disposed. Critics vied to outdo

A riveting, and haunting, snapshot. Dallas, November 22, 1963. Lyndon Johnson, aboard Air Force One, takes the oath of office as 36th president of the United States. *(LBJ Library Collection)*

others' praise. Yet the Great Society was still inchoate; ironically, Barry Goldwater completed it. LBJ's '64 opponent — winning only six states, and 39 percent of the vote — led conservatives to such defeat that Johnson domineered the new Congress. What ensued was Texan — gargantuan. Aid for the poor. Medical care for the aged. Federal aid to education. Finally, the Voting Rights Act: America as meritocracy.

Later, Johnson was dubbed Shakespearean. In early 1965, he made Caesar look like Tom Thumb. Few then had heard of EST, Zen, Spiritualism, Globalism, "Do your own thing," "If it feels good, do it," "Honk if you want peace," or "Don't trust anyone over 30." Who could imagine the horror house that was the mid-to-late-1960s?

Sociologist Robert A. Nisbet has said: "I think it would be difficult to find a single decade in the history of Western culture [of] as much calculated onslaught against culture and convention in any form than the sixties." At Johnson's apex, the irony befit Hamlet. A street-wise meanness began a triumph undreamt of in the suzerainty of Ike and JFK.

REACTION AGAINST THE STRAIGHT-laced 1950s — "obey authority, control your emotions, fit in with the group," a 1991 PBS documentary said, "and don't even think about having sex" — might

have been inevitable. Viet Nam magnified the split. Right v. left. Hard hat against hippie. Main Street v. the '60s radical who opined, "So we struggle, in our humble way, to destroy the United States."

Augury marked Johnson's third day as president. He told a visiting diplomat, "I am not going to be the President who saw South Viet Nam go the way China went." Like Crockett aiding Travis, LBJ rallied to Saigon's side. In August 1964, two U.S. destroyers were attacked in the Gulf of Tonkin. Johnson ordered a counterassault on North Viet Nam. Ike had warned of matching troops "against the teeming millions of Asians." By 1966, LBJ was vowing to nail "that coonskin to the wall."

"I figure that most people believe about 90 percent of what they read," he told aide Bill Moyers. "If I can get the papers to print what I want, most … people will believe me." To cajole, he leaked, flattered, had reporters to dinner, and called at any hour. Nothing sold a strategem — "gradual escalation" — that linked leech-pocked tributaries, soaring casualty rates, and troop commitments that rose from 26,000 to 540,000.

Roosevelt called himself "Dr. Win The War." LBJ dallied between what he termed "the hawks' more war" or "the doves' more peace." Johnson micromanaged the military — yet termed doubters Nervous Nellies. He tried bombing halts and peace sorties — but dropped more U.S. bombs on North Viet Nam than on Germany in World War II. He refused to expand the war to Cambodia and Laos — yet heard "Hey! Hey! LBJ! How many kids did you kill today?" Fudging "guns and butter," he succeeded in losing both.

"We don't want our American boys to do the fighting for Asian boys," he tub-thumped against Goldwater. By February 1965, he was doing what his campaign pledged not to — bombing North Viet Nam. Some saw Johnson's ministry as a singularly revealing nihilism. Others thought the counterculture (that grandiose cliche) unwilling to help an ally (perhaps unable even to know what duty meant).

Which came first — "Credibility Gap" abroad, or "Nightmare on Elm Street" at home? Soon, this Everest presidency seemed lower than Death Valley's floor.

IN 1967, RIOTS TORE DETROIT — 43 died — and in '68, 250 other cities. Bombings, sit-ins, and vandalism marred campuses where panty raids had seemed bravura. Buildings were burned, and scholarly works destroyed. Students tuned in, turned on, and dropped out. Faculties opposed penalties for using marijuana. Academe aped filmmaker Oliver Stone's '90s advice — "Have no fear, make no plans, test and enjoy the limits of life."

By 1968, LBJ could travel only to military bases without fear of protest. Speakers at the 1968 Democratic Convention competed to omit his name. Anti-war protestors fought club-swinging police — crabbed Tom Hayden, "the shock troops of the Establishment." Glass and tear gas confirmed Johnson's March 31 decision to spurn re-election. Seeking unity, LBJ at that moment appeared capable of restoring some honor to the profession of politics.

Johnson's generation had not praised Che Guevara or, miming war's atrocities, struck candles in the night. His America was Iwo Jima, not My-Lai — a remembered hybrid of community and moral superiority. It knew no limits of American power, nor permitted doubt about the power of America's will. "The more trouble they [the Communists] have," Johnson said, "the better for us." He never forgot the lesson of Munich: No one walks away from appeasing an aggressor — he only crawls.

Johnson knew that politics was more intuitive than intellectual. To like you, people must feel they know you. LBJ could eat more, work longer, mimic better, and curse more vividly than any president of our time. He talked to aides while going to the bathroom, had visitors

Late at night, LBJ trooped to the Situation Room to check on casualties in Viet Nam. Here he decorates U.S. troops. "We shall not," he said, "be driven from the battlefield." *(LBJ Library Collection)*

join him naked in his swimming pool, and liked to race his Lincoln convertible around the LBJ Ranch. He also sought to change America as only FDR and Lincoln had.

Many later ascribed Johnson's fall to jiggering that Viet Nam was going well. Or was it, ironically, how he never trusted us to take the real LBJ? *The New York Times'* Charlie Mohr once asked if he had raised his staff's salaries after winning the '64 election. "Well, here you are," Johnson said, "alone with the President of the United States, the leader of the free world, and you ask a chicken

shit question like that." Try moving that to TV! Thus, LBJ hid what he was to project something he was not — pious, somber, and vaguely "presidential."

Six-foot-four, Johnson would squeeze, caress, and nigh molest a visitor — the "Johnson Treatment." Yet there was a compassion, and kindness toward the poor — too, courage, impulsiveness, closeness to wife Lady Bird, and need to be loved. What if he had been judged warts and all — a sagebrush Centurion of the Alamo? Who would have accepted him? Likely more than Johnson thought. When polls dropped, he tried makeup,

Lyndon Baines Johnson Library and Museum. Austin, Texas. In private, Tom Wicker wrote, Johnson was "beyond comparison the most dominant personality I have ever encountered." (*Frank Wolfe*)

contact lenses, and teleprompters. It seemed make-believe, and LBJ a puzzlement. He should have clasped his instincts, after all.

THE BARD OF AVON WROTE, "WHY, man, he doth bestride the narrow world like a Colossus." Texas' grasped his home people's joys, worries, and confessions of the heart. They suffused who Johnson was, and had become, bringing what he knew as a young and restless boy to a world beyond his childhood imaginings.

He mocked the "Ivy Leaguers" and "Harvards" — yet, oddly, yearned for their esteem. Blame insecurity bred of background — Southwest State Normal College and, later, a small-town teacher.

The stiletto lingers of LBJ, as a youth, walking barefoot behind a plow. Perhaps Johnson knew himself too well.

"He was really the history of this country," said Hubert Humphrey, "with all the turmoil, the bombast, the sentiments, the passions." We rarely saw that LBJ — only how he "died of a broken heart," said Richard Nixon after LBJ retired to the Pedernales.

Leave him to poetry, and grateful history. "'A was a man, take him for all in all, I shall not look upon his like again."

Lyndon Baines Johnson Library and Museum. Harry J. Middleton, Director.

2313 Red River Street, Austin, Texas 78705-5702. Phone: (512) 916-5136. Fax: (512) 478-9104. Web site: http://www.lbjlib.utexas.edu.

Visitors have included: Presidents Nixon and Carter. First Ladies Pat Nixon and Betty Ford. Many members of the Johnson administration, including Vice President Hubert Humphrey. Vice President Nelson Rockefeller. Chief Justice Earl Warren. Secretary of State Henry Kissinger. Senator Barry Goldwater. Governor John Connally. General William Westmoreland. Congresswoman Barbara Jordan. Journalist Walter Cronkite. Historian John Kenneth Galbraith. Ann Landers. David and Julie Eisenhower. Actors Kirk Douglas and Gregory Peck. Actresses Carol Channing, Helen Hayes, and Mary Martin. Singer Beverly Sills. Boxer George Foreman.

Hours: Daily, 9 A.M. to 5 P.M. Open every day, except Christmas. Admission: Free. Group tours are urged to make arrangements prior to visit. Free parking. Library gift shop is open during regular hours.

"IT'S ALL HERE — THE STORY OF our time, with the bark off," Lyndon Johnson said by way of dedicating his li-brary and museum. Cynics called it a "Pharaoh's monument." Often thin-skinned about criticism, LBJ might not have disagreed. Its split personality de-fines most presidential centers. The ar-chives stand naked before the scholar. The museum flaunts slant from an ex-travagant/vastness to the landscape/big-ger is better/Texas sort of way.

"If you've been to the Johnson Li-brary only once, you haven't see it," said Gary Yarrington, museum curator from its 1967 groundbreaking to 1996. "If you've been here 25 times, you haven't seen it, because there are additions, and changes, and a special exhibition that just opened." Like Johnson, it is unstaid and populist — the only presidential library with free admission. LBJ never forgot the brace of poverty.

Since its May 22, 1971 dedication, more than 11 million people have visited LBJ's library and museum. Some come for the lode of papers and documents — 40 million-plus pages. Others visit to relive the 1960s. All benefit from the panache of Lady Bird Johnson, who planned the archives. "In my opinion, there should be a melding of both library and museum," she wrote, "from which they would ... become more alive, more vividly used as an instrument to record and remember history."

In her book, *A White House Diary*, Mrs. Johnson relives the two-year crash course she began soon after the 1964

Left, red buckram boxes adorned with the presidential seal dwarf the Great Hall. Its solid walls and open space contrast with the grand staircase, right. *(LBJ Library Collection)*

election. Her first task was to choose a site. LBJ's hometown, Johnson City, and alma mater, Southwest Texas State University, were early leaders. They fell to the University of Texas, which adduced a curricula beyond the library. Today, the Sid W. Richardson Hall houses the LBJ School of Public Affairs, near the library, on a knoll, at the edge of UT's Austin campus.

In 1965-66, Lady Bird toured the libraries of Presidents Hoover, Roosevelt, Truman, and Ike, visited the ancestral homes of other presidents, and studied buildings designed by leading archi-

tects. "I want to use every artistry of ... archivists and staff and family," she said, "to make ours tell the story of our period of time."

Johnson's period, she knew, could be traced to Rebekah Baines Johnson. Like FDR's, LBJ's mother preserved his photos, journals, and scrapbooks from birth through stints as a teacher, congressional aide, and at the National Youth Administration. Today, they flank Johnson's House and Senate papers in the imperial eight-story travertine library above Austin's Waller Creek.

"It's a beautiful building," noted

Yarrington. "But it was designed by an architect [Gordon Bunshaft] who wasn't particularly sympathetic to a museum." Even so, the museum makes you sympathetic to LBJ.

MUSEUM EXHIBITS OCCUPY floors one, two, and eight. LBJ's papers fill floors three through seven. Most archives hide their papers behind closed doors. Not Johnson's. The Great Hall atrium houses four stories of boxes behind a giant glass wall. They are red buckram, embossed with a gold presidential seal, and gawked at by visitors. You can hear the horselaugh of a delighted LBJ.

"These papers are many things," said Harry Middleton, library director and former LBJ speechwriter, "but detached is not among them." e.g. On November 24, 1963, Johnson hadn't moved to the White House — but was working in the Oval Office. Aides at the vice-presidential home were drafting his first speech to Congress. The text trekked back and forth until 3 A.M., when Lady Bird affixed a note to an envelope: "In the name of tomorrow, come eat — then sleep and know you are loved."

Change never sleeps at the LBJ Museum. Since 1971, its permanent exhibits have been redesigned three times. Said Middleton: "Fresh looks are needed as we get further from the president's life."

They start with a first-floor Orientation Theatre video of Johnson's birth in the Hill Country to his burial there 65 years later. Then comes the newest library redesign, "America 1908-69" — which ferries LBJ from his first teaching job in Cotulla to Congress, marriage to Lady Bird, a paper-thin 1941 Senate defeat, 87-vote victory in 1948, and Johnson's years as senator, majority leader, vice president, and president.

"We tell the story of LBJ and Lady Bird in the context of their time," Middleton said. "As the young century

In 1964, America chanted, "All the way with LBJ!" Among the museum's political memorabilia are signets from Johnson's '64 obliteration of Barry Goldwater. (*LBJ Library Collection*)

A 50-foot-long photoengraved mural displays the national elective offices held by Lyndon Johnson and the presidents under whom he served. Its creator was Naomi Savage. *(LBJ Library Collection)*

unfolds, and the U.S. goes to war, the Johnsons are wending their way to a marriage that will leave its mark on history. Later, World War II and the Cold War form the backdrop as LBJ moves up in Congress to become the Senate's most effective leader." Next, the JFK years, with Johnson as veep. Photographs, letters, music, and commentary link key stages of LBJ's, and America's, life: 1908-1919, '20-29, '29-40, '41-45, '46-53, '54-61, and 1961-63.

This redesign leads to "America's" final stage — "1963-69" — starting with the dark corridor of Dallas. Captions, quoting Lady Bird, appear in white on a black wall of photos of Kennedy's presidential motorcade. Leave the corridor, and see why David Halberstam termed LBJ the 20th-Century president "most reeking of human juices." They overflowed in his first days as president — notably, in anti-poverty and civil rights.

The museum catches LBJ's hyperactivity: "Let us continue," he told the Congress. Haunting to a visitor are the portrait of a poor girl by Mel Roman, and mix of signs, photos — "Whites only!" "Colored out!" — and sculpted marchers, allies, and freedom riders. Ralph Ellison later wrote that LBJ might have to settle for being the greatest president for the poor and black — "but that, in itself, is a very great honor indeed."

HONORABLE, AND INDELIBLE, were the music of the Righteous Brothers, black rhetoric demanding the right to vote, Carol Channing's "Hello, Dolly," and LBJ taking the oath of office on Air Force One. All dot the 1963-69 exhibit. Closeby artifacts recall the deaths of Robert Kennedy and Dr. Martin Luther King, Jr., LBJ's War on Poverty, Mrs. Johnson's charm, aplomb, and campaign to beautify America, and the '60s culture war: Walls note Peter Max's art, go-go dancers, the model Twiggy, and the film, *The Graduate* — and gnawing involvement in Viet Nam.

See photos of the Viet Namese attack on the USS *Maddox* in the Gulf of Tonkin; a 500-pound bomb, dropped in Operation Rolling Thunder, in a corner of the museum; and bas relief soldiers against a pictorial battlefield: "The War That Broke America's Will." Read how LBJ confided to Lady Bird, "I can't get out [of Viet Nam]. I can't finish it with what I have got. So what the hell can I do?"

What Johnson did is evinced by "The Thousand Laws of the Great Society." Its display links statutes from the Job Corps to Medicare — and hundreds of pens Johnson used to sign, say, Head Start, the Voting Rights Act, and federal aid to education. Nearby are the "Hot

Line" teletype machine that wired LBJ to foreign countries and teleprompter print-out from March 31, 1968. "Accordingly, I shall not seek, and I will not accept, the nomination of my party for another term as your president."

Like the Johnson presidency, the first floor ends with poignance in its wings. Hubert Humphrey is nominated for president, and Richard Nixon elected. LBJ leaves Washington for return to his Texas

Bronze portraits of President and Mrs. Johnson grace the museum. Robert Berks sculpted them in the Johnsons' last month in the White House — January 1969. *(LBJ Library Collection)*

Elizabeth Shoumatoff's portrait of FDR hangs above the mantelpiece of the re-created Oval Office. Note the custom-built coffee table with call directory telephone. *(LBJ Library Collection)*

ranch. For surcease, pass a 1910 Model T that Henry Ford II gave to LBJ, Lincoln stretch limousine flying the presidential flag and Stars and Stripes, and archives visible from the staircase, and climb to the second floor. Hear "The Humor of LBJ" — Johnson on a deaf whiskey lover, or little boy who mistakes the family dog for a lion. Yawp at "America's Handiwork" — gifts from the *cognoscenti*. A Steuben donkey, lobster trap model, beagles made of egg cartons and orange felt, and Bowie knife are as different as the way people saw LBJ.

To aide Jack Valenti, Johnson was "an avalanche of a man." His snowslide crowds floor two. Lighted "Head of State Gifts" complement the domestic presents: ceremonial swords from King Hassan II and King Faisal, a first-century marble bust from the president of Italy, and a Chinese tomb sculpture (618-908 A.D.) from Chiang Kai-shek. A few feet away the First Lady's Theatre shows a 57-minute film — "A Life: The Story of Lady Bird Johnson," by Charles Guggenheim — and copies of official White House portraits of Martha Washington through Barbara Bush.

Valenti called LBJ "an awesome engine of a man … towering, endlessly. Mesmerizing." Next door is an exhibit — "American Political Memorabilia" — the political animal would have loved. Dote on the coverlet of presidential voices — FDR's pitch, or the tones of Harding and Calvin Coolidge. Study the changing exhibits — Ulysses Grant, or the 1920s and '30s. Be regaled by the more than 4,000 political campaign trinkets in the Ralph E. Becker collection. Tired, or jaded? Get in the elevator, push a button, and enter a 1965 Twilight Zone of time.

THE MUSEUM'S MOST POPULAR exhibit — an Oval Office replica — lies on the eighth, or top, floor. Its seven-eighths scale prevents things like LBJ's curved television console from being shown. What incongruity: a smaller-than-life office for this larger-than-life man.

"There's an obvious tendency to think in shrinelike terms when you begin one of these," said Middleton. "But that kind of thinking flattens after a while." Around a corner, Lady Bird extends the process with a tour of public and private rooms of the executive mansion — especially the Treaty Room, where planning for the LBJ Library began.

"You see what you expect to see here," said Yarrington, "something about LBJ, his Presidency, and the '60s. But this is also a museum of American history." Returning to the first floor, you spy the start of "America 1908-1969" — with William Howard Taft as president, Thomas Edison's invention of the movie machine, and Admiral Peary reaching the North Pole.

"And there's a birth out in the Hill Country," Yarrington added. "It's LBJ — he's just a baby. He didn't have anything to do with any of it, but he was born and we acknowledge that."

We all do at the LBJ Library and Museum.

★ ★ ★

Dedication excerpts, May 22, 1971.

"Just a few minutes ago, as President

Johnson was throwing me [laughter] — showing me through the library — I am coming back later when I have more time [laughter] — we visited what I think may prove to be the most exciting and popular room in the whole library for the visitor, a replica of the Oval Office."— Richard Nixon

"A President sees things from a unique perspective. No one can share his responsibility. No can can share the scope of his duties or the burden of his decisions. In my book, I explain: 'I have not written these chapters to say, "This is how it was," but to say, "This is how I saw it from my vantage point." ' "
— Lyndon Johnson

"It has been my privilege, during a quarter-century of public service, to know many partisans of principle. I think today especially of those times during the Eisenhower Administration, when I was Vice President and Lyndon Johnson was the Majority Leader of the United States Senate. He was a vigorous leader of his party. But I knew, and President Eisenhower often told me, and he knew, that whenever the great issues of national security were concerned, he would always be a partisan of principle, not a partisan of party. That is Lyndon Baines Johnson."— Richard Nixon

"A Presidential Library is many things.

It is the past: millions of documents ... all preserving some fragments of a time gone by. It is the present: a melding of library and museum, filled with the voices of tourists, yet providing quiet retreats for scholars. Most of all, it is the future: a place where the judgment of history will be made."— Lyndon Johnson

Directions: From the North, take Interstate 35 south to Austin. Exit west on 26th Street. Go south on Red River Street and follow signs to the LBJ Library and Museum. From the East, go west on Martin Luther King Boulevard, which becomes 19th Street. Proceed north on Red River Street to the library and museum. From the South, take I-35 north. Exit west on 19th Street. Go north on Red River Street to the library and museum. From the West, go east on 19th Street. Exit north on Red River Street to the library and museum.

LBJ, returning to the Hill Country, January 20, 1969. He wrote of the presidency: "I knew I had been there. And I knew also that I had given it everything that was in me." *(Charles Phillips, TIME Inc.)*

CHAPTER 11

THOROUGHLY MODERN MILHOUS
RICHARD NIXON LIBRARY
AND BIRTHPLACE

(Richard Nixon Library and Birthplace)

THE TOWN WHERE I GREW UP — Caledonia, New York [Pop. 2,188] — had one bar, six churches, and no traffic lights. Its people believed in work, God, family, a fondness for the familiar, and a reverence for everything American. Their hero was not JFK nor beloved Ike but the quintessence of Middle America. In Richard Nixon, they found what their parents and grandparents — bullied by a ruling class John Anderson dubbed the "Volvo and brie cheese crowd" — had rarely known. A Voice.

Disdaining pluralistic ignorance, where the members of a Majority — theirs; the Silent — felt outflanked, it seemed natural to admire Nixon's hardscrabble life. "No matter what you say," gibed Jimmy Carter in 1976, "he was a leader." He regarded "trendies" and "beautiful people" and "academics who couldn't butter a piece of toast" as something akin to the Bubonic plague.

Meg Greenfield wrote of the "Nixon Generation." After Watergate forced RN to resign, aide Bryce Harlow likened him to a bobbed cork. Push Nixon down — always, he resurfaced. Only FDR ran as many times for national office: five. More people voted for him for president than any man in history. In post-World War II America, his history was our history. Nixon 'R' Us.

TO ME, NIXON BEGAN IN THE MOST theatric election of our time. I recall 1960 vividly and how even after the Great Debates — my mother saying of the first, "He [Nixon] looks terrible" — and the swirl of its final weeks — Kennedy stumping the Northeast; a countering Nixon telethon — it was unthinkable to a nine-year-old Republican that Kennedy would win.

Election Night went quickly, for I was asleep before 8 — Nixon ahead, but Kennedy gaining. Next morning I raced to the door and grabbed Gannett's then-flagship paper, the Rochester, New York,

In 1958, then-Vice President and Mrs. Nixon were stoned and almost killed by mobs in Caracas. They were greeted as heroes by President Eisenhower, left, in Washington. *(Nixon Library)*

Democrat & Chronicle. The headline screamed disaster: "Kennedy Wins." (The subhead was cheerier: "Nixon Carries Monroe County.")

In 1962, Nixon lost to Pat Brown for governor of California. Incinerated, mocked as a loser, derided for his squareness, he amazed by becoming a candidate for the 1968 GOP nomination. The reason foretold his presidency. There was nostalgia and love — akin to a gentle protectiveness — for Pat's cloth coats and the Nixon family, decent, much-wounded, and as straight and resolute as they came.

Upstate New York saw Nixon as brave and vulnerable and thoughtful and sentimental. It was a view so divorced from Washington's as to rival a dialogue of the deaf.

IN 1967, I MAILED A HANDWRITten letter to the senior partner at the Manhattan law firm of Nixon, Mitchell, Mudge, and Rose. I was president of my church's Ecumenical Fellowship and our group would be in New York in August and was there the slightest chance I could meet him and, if there was, it would be as grand as anything I had known.

In early April I received an answer from his secretary, Rose Woods. Nixon would be out of the country, writing for *Reader's Digest*. However, schedules change, and would I call upon arrival. I

did, and was invited to Nixon's office at 20 Broad Street, off Wall, a world and *Weltanschauung* from Upstate New York. For half an hour we talked of sports and college — Nixon suggested Cornell: "thank God, the least Ivy of the Ivies" — and the psychic need to work your way through school.

I still think fondly of how Nixon need not have met me but did, as a kindness. Later, I was to find this typical not of the Old nor New but Real Nixon — shy and solicitous. I did not know this at the time. Two years later I entered college as he took the oath of office. It was then, as America set herself in belligerence, that Nixon fused person and president like no chief executive since FDR.

It is hard for post-Baby Boomers to grasp how early-1970s America seemed at once alive, passionate, and coming apart at the seams. Upheaval tinged values and morality, civil rights, feminism, drugs, whether police were pigs, love should be free and grades abolished, and America — as George McGovern said — should "come home." The University of Pennsylvania avoided confrontation with student war protestors by removing its American flags to storage. Jane Fonda went to North Viet Nam, and thundered against "those blue-eyed murderers — Nixon and the rest of those ethnocentric American white male chauvinists."

On April 30, 1970, vowing that

America would not be "a pitiful, helpless giant," Nixon announced the invasion of Cambodia. Campuses exploded when six students were murdered at Kent State University and Jackson State College. Hundreds of schools closed or went on strike. Buses ringed the White House to ward off protestors. Hawk confronted dove. Alumni fought student body. Peoria felt besieged.

NIXON UPHELD IT LESS THROUGH policy than personality. His programs were often moderate: welfare reform,

revenue sharing, the All-Volunteer Army, the EPA. Despite Viet Nam, he engaged in diplomatic summitry and helped end the bipolar world. In February 1972, Nixon ended decades of estrangement in the primordial world of Peking, Hang-chow, and the Forbidden City. Later, he became the first U.S. president to visit Moscow — joining Communist Party leader Leonid Brezhnev in the first agreement of the nuclear age to limit strategic nuclear arms.

Nixon loved foreign policy — glo-bal, conceptual, moving chessmen from

Nixon, flashing thumbs up, on the morning of his 1990 library dedication. He remains perhaps the most compelling figure of post-World War II America. *(The Orange County Register)*

a distance. He was more direct fighting America's cultural war. My generation loved the amplified beat of rock. Said Nixon at a White House dinner with Fred Waring and the Pennsylvanians, "If the music's square, it's because I like it square." The liberal elite adored nothing if not fads. Nixon liked sports, hated cocktail parties, despised "front-runners, the social climbers," and thumbed his nose at the fashionable. "My family never had the wild, swinging times many trendies think of," he told me. "What we did have, of course, was a lot of fun. I, for example, and depending on the season, naturally, loved to sit down and belt out some Christmas carols."

Mid-America could see Nixon as Father Christmas and not be deceived. That is why it could accept what a top aide, Raymond Price, called Nixon's "dark side" — the taped Milhous of "expletive deleted" — knowing that his good eclipsed the bad. He wore the flag in his lapel pin, disdained draft-dodgers as "idealistic? What they wanted was to protect their ass," and grasped the Forgotten American's nobility and injury. "Farmers. Shopkeepers," a PBS documentary said. "People with an inbred respect for authority and an unyielding belief in the American Dream." Mocked by the maniacal '60s, they felt not bigotry but hurt pride. Nixon gave them what the Eastern Establishment withheld

— a decent measure of respect.

Nixon's public lay among the ordered and traditional — "good, law-abiding, tax-paying citizens." Duty mattered. To them, Viet Nam was a test of character — whether the U.S. stood by an ally or left it to stand alone. Too, religion. Once, Nixon told aide Charles Colson, "You know, I could be a Catholic. I honestly could. It's beautiful to think about, that there is something you can really grab ahold of, something real and meaningful."

Even Nixon's awkwardness played in Winesburg, Ohio. It was unslick, endearing. At RN's July 19, 1990 library

Before Nixon went to China or negotiated with the Soviets, he tried to end the Viet Nam War. In 1969, his first year as president, RN went to Asia to visit U.S. troops. *(Nixon Library)*

dedication, George Bush told how one afternoon at an airport Nixon heard a little girl shouting, "How is Smokey the Bear?" — at that time living in the Washington Zoo. Nixon smiled as the girl kept repeating her question. Baffled, he turned to an aide for translation. "Smokey the Bear, Mr. President," the aide whispered. "Washington Zoo." Triumphant, Nixon walked over, took the girl's hand, and beamed, "How do you do, Miss Bear?"

NIXON'S FLAWS, FANS SAW AS virtues. His virtues, critics saw as sins. His solitude, they termed isolation; his reserve, arrogance; his propriety, aloofness; his sentimentality, corn. Nixon as Grant Wood *v.* the age's fashion embodied Greenfield's "traumatic clash of cultures." As it lodged in the White House, in a man who despised — and was despised by — America's hip, camp, and pop art intelligentsia, it split families, politicians, above all, generations, and cemented his rapport with America's great middle masses before helping to bring about his fall.

Ironically, Nixon had an intellectual's complexity. He liked nuance, respected the writing craft, and authored 10 books — six best-sellers. Once, he told Price, "I am an introvert in an extrovert's profession." Yet he became the tribune of people who never read *The New York Times*. His

goal was a new political, even cultural, majority. He almost made it. Instead, his triumphs graced office photos that catapulted back a visitor — Nixon with Meir or Brezhnev; Nixon in Peking; Nixon speaking, waving, deplaning; Nixon in a motorcade, with Pat, flinging high the V.

When I left college, the shadow on those walls was a president seeking to reshape the world — bold yet retiring, believing that "politics is poetry, not prose." When last I saw him, in 1990, he was frail and hunched. He quizzed me about the Bush administration, and suggested that I run for Congress. He was wary of raising taxes, supportive of Bush in the Gulf, and proud of the woman whose Secret Service code was "Starlight" — his wife of 53 years.

Pat Nixon overcame tragedy to become a mirror of America's heart, and love. Is it coincidence that by 10 months his death followed hers? In March 1991, on the eve of Mrs. Nixon's 79th birthday, I took to their New Jersey home a giant card arrayed with photos of her life and signatures of more than 200 White House staffers. Unpacking it, I pled for patience: "I'm the most unmechanical person you'll meet." Playfully, she replied, "No you're not. Dick is." I had never met Mrs. Nixon. For two hours we spoke of family, work, and travel. It was like talking to your own mother.

Later, Nixon wrote to call it "the

Above all, Nixon sought to be a peacemaker. Among White House visitors was Israeli Prime Minister Golda Meir. A successor, Yitzak Rabin, can be seen at Nixon's right. *(Nixon Library)*

most memorable birthday card she has ever received." Asked once what word would engrave his heart if it were opened after he died, he said, simply, "Pat."

A favorite picture showed them on a bench, in San Clemente, gazing at the Pacific. Her head rests on the shoulder of the man who extolled freedom and security and, campaigning, upheld "peace without surrender" and "the spiritual values of America" and who each election, as autumn dawned, communed with rallies in the rain — the most remarkable American of our time.

Richard Nixon Library and Birthplace. John Taylor, Director. 18001 Yorba Linda Boulevard, Yorba Linda, California 92686. Phone: (714) 993-5075. Fax: (714) 528-0544. Web site: www.chapman. edu/nixon.

Visitors have included: Presidents Ford, Carter, Reagan, Bush, and Clinton. First Ladies Lady Bird Johnson, Betty Ford, Rosalynn Carter, Nancy Reagan, Barbara Bush, and Hillary Clinton. Leading members of the Nixon Administration. Vice President Dan Quayle. Secretary of State Henry Kissinger. Senator Bob Dole. Governor Pete Wilson. Mrs. Anwar Sadat. British Prime Minister Edward Heath. Evangelist Billy Gra-

ham. Actors Buddy Ebsen, Bob Hope, Charlton Heston, and Arnold Schwarzenegger.

Hours: Monday through Saturday, 10 A.M. to 5 P.M. Sunday, 11 A.M. to 5 P.M. Open every day, except New Year's Day, Thanksgiving, and Christmas. Admission: Children age 7 and under, free. Children age 8 to 11, $1. Adults age 12 and over, $4.95. Seniors age 62 and over, $2.95. Special rates of 20 or more with advance reservations. Call (714) 993-3393. Free parking. Library gift shop is open during regular hours.

Richard Nixon Materials Staff. Karl Weissenback, Acting Director. National Archives at College Park, 8601 Adelphi Road, College Park, Maryland 20740. Phone: (301) 713-6950. Fax: (301) 713-6916. Web site: http://gopher. nora.gov:70/1/inform/library/nixon.

Hours: Monday and Wednesday, 8:45 A.M. to 5 P.M., Tuesday, Thursday, and Friday, 8:45 to 9 P.M., Saturday, 8:45 to 4:45 P.M. Requests to use records after 5 P.M. must be submitted no later than 3:30 P.M. that day and by 3:30 P.M. on Friday for Saturday use. Listening hours for the Nixon tapes are Monday through Friday, 8:45 A.M. to 4 P.M. Free parking.

Richard Nixon Library and Birthplace. Yorba Linda, California. Said Henry Kissinger of RN: "Few men so needed to be loved and were so shy about the grammar of love." *(Nixon Library)*

RICHARD NIXON SAID THAT "PRESI-dential libraries can be dry, deadly, dull places, full of memoranda no one reads when they were written and only archivists will read in the future." By contrast, Nixon wanted his library to let "new generations of Americans ... see how in America a boy born in a tiny farmhouse his father built can somebody be President."

The Nixon Library is muted and unassuming — nearer Truman's, say, than Kennedy's white stark edifice against a 112-foot-high atrium of black glass above Boston Harbor. An architectural critic said the library "makes it hard to believe that Mr. Kennedy was anything but a man of energy, of zest, of confidence." Nixon's would leave you thinking of scholarship, and courage.

The library took two decades to build. RN's first choice, in Yorba Linda, abutted the simple house of his birth. Ironically, his father's once-orange grove now housed a school there named after Nixon as vice president! Spurned, he looked elsewhere. In 1970, Whittier College bid, then retreated after Watergate. Later, faculty bad blood led Nixon's law school — Duke University — and UC Irvine to withdraw.

Would Nixon's library become the Flying Dutchman? In 1984, San Clemente okayed a site on a bluff

"Road to the Presidency" re-creates a 1950 campaign rally, with 1949 Mercury "Woody" station wagon. Nixon stumped California, giving speeches from the wagon's tailgate. *(Nixon Library)*

overlooking RN's Western White House. Next, a four-year delay. Finally, in 1987 Yorba Linda closed its elementary school, at which point the land became available, whereupon the Nixon Foundation agreed to restore RN's birthplace and open it as part of a presidential library.

Richard Nixon would tell you: He never got anything for free.

QUICKLY, ROADBLOCKS YIELDED to limits scorned. The foundation built the library privately for $25 million. Groundbreaking occurred in 1989. Said President Bush at the July 1990 dedication of Nixon's goal of a generation of peace: "History will say of you: 'Here was a true architect of peace.'"

The Victorians called serene, cloudless spells "Queen's Weather." The nine-acre Nixon Library opened to presidents' weather as the Nixons, Bushes, Reagans, and Fords, and cypress, palms, and eucalyptus hailed a life not of *Six Crises* but a single crisis — heroic and/or abhorrent, often, unbelievable — and the only library, except Hayes', operated without federal funds.

Yorba Linda ties a Spanish-style main gallery and archives, 293-seat theatre, 75-seat amphitheatre, 3,000-square foot reflecting pool, and First Lady's

Garden. Its 52,000 square feet house memorabilia — Nixon made *TIME* magazine's cover a record 66 times — and film, exhibit, interactive video, photo, re-creation, and Reading Room on the lower floor.

Here the most complete record available on Nixon's life and time runs through a course of congressional, campaign, vice-presidential, and out-of-office files, private diaries and pre-presidential papers, book manuscripts, foreign correspondence, key presidential documents, and papers donated by other members of his administration. Eventu-

ally, the core collection will also include RN's post-presidential papers.

"Welcome to our academic heartbeat," said John Taylor, former Nixon aide and 1990- library director. "What a galaxy — the '60 presidential strategy, RN's association with John Kennedy or J. Edgar Hoover, or U.S. relations with Latin America." Sadly, the brightest star is missing: Nixon's presidential papers and tapes, three thousand miles away, in suburban Washington, D.C.

Nixon signed a post-resignation agreement with the General Services Administration: White House tapes, and

In the late 1980s, Nixon's boyhood farmhouse was moved to its original location, restored, and now lies adjacent to the library. The Nixons' gravesites lie nearby. *(Nixon Library)*

The Structure of Peace Gallery, left, recalls Nixon's foreign policy. At right, statues hail persons who met his criterion of leadership: "Did they make a difference?" *(Nixon Library)*

some presidential papers, would be destroyed. Congress countered with a law giving the material to the federal government. Its custodian, the National Archives in College Park, Maryland, has already released many papers and sent copies to Yorba Linda.

Alas, they are not real McCoys. The library is still seeking the originals in court. Released, they would light Nixon's entire galaxy — to Taylor, a scholar's "necessary and sufficient stop."

IT IS NECESSARY, BUT NOT SUFFI-cient, to visit the library's Watergate display. Viewers hear tapes of the coverup, and view RN's last days as president. By

then, they have seen the movie, *Never Give Up: Richard Nixon in the Arena* — and begun exhibits from Checkers via the Great Debates through the Great Comeback to Elba West.

"Let history record that we just did not save the world from communism," Nixon said, "but that we helped make the world safe for freedom." The library's world starts with childhood photos, letters, essays, and Pat and Dick's early correspondence. Next are marriage, the Navy, RN's return to peacetime, Congress, and a hollowed-out pumpkin, microfilm, microphone, and Woodstock typewriter — a.k.a. Nixon *v.* convicted perjurer Alger Hiss.

A few feet away stands "Road to the Presidency." Espy the 1949 Mercury "Woody" station wagon that Nixon used to stump for the '50 U.S. Senate — or 1951 meeting with Ike that spawned his vice presidency. View *LIFE* magazine 1960 campaign photos, TV debates unhorsing Nixon in a '60s-style living room, and memorabilia of its candidates and America — small towns, whistle stops, and big-city rallies.

"Visitors know 1960," said Taylor. "What surprises is what comes next" — the 1961-68 wilderness. Return to California, 1962 run for governor, travel, and law practice. The exhibit details 1968's black activism, women's and anti-war movements, Peoria on parade, and melting pot of a campaign. Election night swayed back and forth — Nixon ahead, then Humphrey, and finally RN. Elected, foreign policy became Nixon's grail.

The library airs life-sized statues and videos of 10 famous 20th-Century leaders in conversation. A touch sensitive video monitor rekindles Charles de Gaulle, Konrad Adenauer, Winston Churchill, Yoshida Shigeru, Anwar Sadat, Golda Meir, Chou En-lai, Mao Tse-tung, Nikita Khrushchev, and Leonid Brezhnev — presenting a biographical sketch of the leader, the story of his or her relationship with Nixon, and quotations from both.

Photos describe the "backchannel communication" that led to 1972's trip to the People's Republic of China. A "typical" American tract home recalls Viet Nam, peace with honor, and POWs coming home. For 20 years, Nixon dueled Soviet leadership. "Onion domes" like those at Moscow's St. Basil's evoke the 1959 "Kitchen Debate" with Khrushchev and 1972 first U.S. president-to-address-the-Soviet people speech.

"Americans," said RN, "elect a President for foreign policy." His belief endures at Yorba Linda like the rhythms of the Thames.

President and Mrs. Nixon at the wedding of daughter Tricia, June 12, 1971. (*Nixon Library*)

A PRIVATE MAN, NIXON PREFER-
red the Lincoln Sitting Room to Oval Office. His favorite place is re-created
from the White House family quarters.
Also: RN's domestic policies, 1972
demolition of George McGovern, and interactive state-of-the-art video. Ask a
question, and hear Nixon's instant on-
screen answer. You decide whether it is
"perfectly clear."

Equally Outer Space are the pistol
Elvis Presley gave RN and moon rock
and telephone he used to talk to Apollo
11 astronauts on the moon. Radiant is
the 36-by-96 foot reflecting pool which

forms the U-shaped library. To the east
lie the Citrus Garden, Formal Garden,
and First Lady's Garden — and, inside,
the rail display above them for the
woman who made America *en famille*.

Pat Nixon hailed volunteerism, arranged White House outside lighting, began the Right to Read and Parks to
People programs, and was the most traveled First Lady. Displays include her
second inaugural gown, red suit worn in
China, and Nixon's favorite photo of
himself and Pat — in the Rose Garden
for Tricia's wedding, June 12, 1971.

Winston Churchill said of Prime

The Lincoln Sitting Room, Nixon's favorite room in the White House family quarters. The library re-
creates it, with RN's actual armchair and ottoman. *(Nixon Library)*

Minister Asquith, "His children are his best memorial." Nixon's binds a U.S. commemorative stamp with first-day-of issue (April 26, 1995), plaque denoting his Center for Peace and Freedom, and private study as it was April 18, 1994, the day he suffered a fatal stroke. The alcove includes his desk, easy chair, ottoman, telephone table, and leather briefcase, with notes for remarks Nixon planned for his grandson's ninth-grade graduation.

Temporary exhibits complete the mix. Christmas cards from Ike through Clinton. Letters between RN and JFK. Displays honor the 200th anniversary of the White House — "Farewell, Mr.

The Gallup Poll calls Pat Nixon among the most admired women of post-war USA. *(Nixon Library)*

President": The week of Nixon's stroke is etched by photomural, get-well notes, and the flag from RN's casket — and "Rockin' the White House: Four decades of Presidents and popular music."

Watch Nixon at the National Press Club in 1960, playing the piano to Jack Benny's violin. Even Nixon-haters will concede that music endures all.

THE *BOSTON GLOBE* WROTE THAT "He emerges as the one true superstar of the 1970s." Your tour ends with the house his father built. Nixon's voice describes life in the farmhouse, restored with original family furniture, including the piano he played as a boy.

RN oversaw the revival — his, and the home's. He recalled the living room with piano next to the bedroom doorway; kitchen, with wood-burning stove, icebox, sink, and highchair; and adjacent room where his mother spent hours canning and preparing meals. In his parents' room is the bed (and 1875 quilt used to cover it) on which Nixon was born.

Upstairs is off-limits — its stairway too fragile for foot traffic. Still, RN wanted his boyhood room restored. The cramped attic lot where he and his brothers slept had two beds, chest, chair, and built-in shelf used as a desk. Photos show why Nixon said there was hardly any room in there to turn around.

"I know what it means to be poor,"

Nixon's *Memoirs* began: "I was born in the house my father built." RN's boyhood home is open to the public. Note the desk, music stand, and dinner table — in one room. *(Nixon Library)*

he said. You take him at his word in a house reputedly ordered from the Sears catalogue. The 900-square-foot home lacks a bathtub and is so tiny that almost the entire ground floor can be viewed from the living room. Even the same pepper and palm trees still shade the site.

"He's our last log cabin President," said historian Stephen Ambrose. A most unusual library, and man.

★ ★ ★

Dedication excerpts, July 19, 1990.

"What you will see here, among other things, is a personal life. The influence of a strong family, of inspirational ministers, of great teachers. You will see a political life, running for Congress, running for the Senate, running for governor, running for president three times. And you will see the life of a great nation; 77 years of it. A period in which we had unprecedented progress for the United States. And you will see great leaders, leaders who changed the world, who helped to make the world what we have today." — Richard Nixon

"Richard Nixon is a man who understands the world. He understands politics, power, and the forces of history. Whether with Mao or Brezhnev, de Gaulle or Gandhi, President Nixon was the first among equals. During my eight years in the White House, I relied on his insight and wisdom, and I will always be grateful for the benefit of his seasoned expertise." — Ronald Reagan

"Tomorrow, the first visitors will enter our newest Presidential Library ... They will hear of Horatio Alger and Alger Hiss. Of the book, Six Crises, *and the seventh crisis, Watergate. They will think of Checkers — Millie's role model. And, yes, Mr. President, they will hear again your answer to my 'vision thing' — 'Let me make this perfectly clear.'"* — George Bush

"If you take no risks, you will suffer no defeats. But without risks, you will win no victories. You must never be satisfied with success, and you should never be

July 19, 1990 was clearly a Republican day. Four GOP presidents — Reagan, Nixon, Bush, and Ford — gathered in the main lobby before touring the library and birthplace. *(David Valdez)*

discouraged by failure. Failure can be sad. But the greatest sadness is not to try and fail, but to fail to try at all. Only when you become engaged in a cause greater than yourself, can you be true to yourself." — Richard Nixon

Library Directions: From Los Angeles, go south on Interstate 5. Exit east at Highway 91 and proceed to Highway 57. Exit north and go to Yorba Linda Boulevard. Exit east to the Nixon Library and Birthplace. From San Diego, go north

on I-5 to Highway 57. Exit north and go to Yorba Linda Blvd. Exit east to the library and birthplace. From Anaheim, take Katella Avenue to Highway 57. Go north to Yorba Linda Blvd, and exit east. From Riverside and San Bernadino, take Highway 91 to Imperial Highway (Highway 90). Exit north on Imperial Highway and go to Yorba Linda Blvd. Proceed left to the library and birthplace.

Archives Directions: From the North, take Interstate 95 south. Exit west at Interstate 495 (Capital Beltway). Exit south on New Hampshire Avenue. Go east on

The library features Nixon's private study, as it was April 18, 1994, the day he suffered his fatal stroke. Handwritten letters and speech notes are on his desk and tables. *(Nixon Library)*

Nixon often lauded "peace at the center." Perhaps he found it as a Joint Services Military Honor Guard escorted RN's flag-draped casket to April 27, 1994 burial — next to Pat. *(Nixon Library)*

Adelphi Road. Turn left at the National Archives. From the East, take I-495 west. Exit south on New Hampshire Avenue. Go east on Adelphi Road. Turn left at archives. From the South, take New Hampshire Avenue north. Go east on Adelphi Road. Turn left at archives. From the West, take I-495 east. Exit south on New Hampshire Avenue. Go east on Adelphi Road. Turn left at archives.

CHAPTER 12

I SAW THE LIGHT

PLAY WORD-ASSOCIATION about U.S. presidents. LBJ — Hercules with Achilles' heel. Truman — a bantam rooster, ordinary and extraordinary. Did Nixon denote gaping insecurity, or demonic courage? Is it right to paint Kennedy as Boston-Ivy-Navy-"vigah"-Peace Corps-money-looks?

Yes, or no? It depends on whom you talk to. Gerald Ford was an accident, or nice guy who finished first. Norman Mailer scored Ronald Reagan's "tripped-on-my shoelaces, aw-shucks variety of confusion." Was he wrong? Will history write that Jimmy Carter was too good for the office, or just good enough?

In 1861, leaving Springfield, Illinois, to assume the presidency, Lincoln told his home people, "The great God which helped General Washington must help me. Without that great assistance, I will surely fail. With it, I cannot fail."

Presidents vary, yet share the idea we call America. Below are library photos of Ford, Carter, Reagan, and George Bush — leaders who despaired of failing God, and man.

Gerald R. Ford Library. Ann Arbor, Michigan. *(Ford Library)*

Jimmy Carter Library. Atlanta, Georgia. *(Carter Library)*

Ronald Reagan Library and Museum. Simi Valley, California. *(Reagan Library)*

George Bush Library and Museum. College Station, Texas. *(Texas A&M University)*

CHAPTER 13

JERRY, BE GOOD
GERALD R. FORD LIBRARY
AND MUSEUM

(Per Kjeldsen)

AMERICA IN THE WAKE OF

Watergate had a quirky, scattered feel.

Leisure suits dressed a gender, 29 persons died of a mysterious ailment called "Legionnaire's Disease," and with a burst of fireworks a million people celebrated the country's 200th birthday by watching a grand flotilla of tall ships in New York Harbor. *Taxi Driver* and *Rocky* buoyed theatres. Americans found passing fancy in discomania and citizens band radio. Chicago authored "If You Leave Me Now," a lambent ode to lost faith. One man set out straightaway to raise America's.

"What have you learned about politics?" a student once asked.

"That you should have a healthy

dichotomy," I said. "I like politics and dislike most politicians."

Gerald Ford was an exception. He braved politics as a nice man in an egomaniac's craft. He struck you as stoic, solid, and impressed with policy, but not himself. Ford's humility sacked by contrast the capital's hacks, flacks, charlatans, and shills. He treated pomp the way Billy Graham did sin.

James Fenimore Cooper wrote, "Truth was the Deerslayer's polar star." It lit Ford's "Here the people rule," "Ours is a country of laws, not men," and "Honesty is the best policy in the end." Lyndon Johnson erred by calling Ford

"the only guy too dumb to walk and chew gum at the same time." Perhaps it's hard to grasp a pol who said what he meant — and meant what he said.

Ford calmed our quiet desperation. Who among us wouldn't say, right man, right time? America's 38th president was Michigan '35. Trusting him remains as natural as his booing Ohio State.

FORD'S LIFE HAS BEEN TOLD LESS often than Lincoln's or even Jimmy Carter's. Leslie Lynch King, Jr., was born on Bastille Day 1913, in Omaha, then moved to Grand Rapids when his parents divorced. His mother married

President Ford, with officials including Secretary of State Henry Kissinger. Said Ford: "Trust is the glue that holds our government together." *(Ford Library)*

Gerald Rudolph Ford. Adopted, the child took Ford's name.

Ford soon became a Boy Scout, and earned the rank of Eagle Scout. Parents fantasize about their child becoming president. Ford wished to be the next Red Grange. As president, he relived his existential pleasure as a 1930s football player by reading the sports section first. "Thanks to football, I knew the value of team play," he explained. "It is, I believe, one of the most important lessons to be learned and practiced in our lives."

One lesson was life's plots and turns. Leaving Michigan, Ford spurned pro football — the Packers and Lions offered him a job — to attend Yale, become a model, go to and back from war, practice law in Grand Rapids, and in 1948 marry a woman for the half-century still to come. Another lesson: If a politician is good enough, lasts long enough, and is possessed of an easy familiarity, he becomes an extended member of the family.

Elected in '48 by 60.5 percent, Ford began a 25-year skein as Michigan's Sixth District's "Congressman for Life." In 1964, he served on the Warren Commission. In 1965, Ford became House Minority leader, and joined his opposite — the Senate's Everett Dirksen — in the quasi-camp "The Ev and Jerry Show."

Each TV program addressed "The Question of the Week." A sample: "Mr.

President and Mrs. Ford in the White House. In 1976, GOP campaign buttons read: "Vote for Betty's husband." (*Ford Library*)

President: Why is the War on Poverty Being Lost?" Ford backed Johnson in Viet Nam, but thought we pulled our punches. In 1970, he tried to impeach liberal Supreme Court Justice William O. Douglas. Such contretemps were rare. Ford was loyal, temperate, and a Member of The Club. Then, in October 1973, Spiro Agnew resigned as vice president. Richard Nixon wanted John Connally. Instead, he tapped the tortoise, not hare — open, reliable, and sure to be confirmed.

"They like you," Nixon whispered after choosing Ford as Agnew's successor. It was easy to see why. "I'm a Ford, not a Lincoln," he observed, truly and gracefully. Ford's identity greased ability to relate. "Of all the Presidents I've interviewed, Ford was the easiest," said NBC's John Chancellor. "There was a good-guy aura that the country needed. Ford had as few enemies as anyone could possibly have."

On August 9, 1974, Nixon resigned as president. Replacing him, Ford said, "Our long national nightmare is over." Replete with memory is how America soon felt at repose with him.

AWASH IN LIGHT, FORD TYPI-cally tried to dim it. "May Richard Nixon, who brought peace to millions," he said in his swearing-in, "find it for himself." The new president found a go-ings-on of crisis. Recession: unemployment hit 7.1 percent. Inflation: Ford vowed, "Whip Inflation Now" — WIN.

Ford, at a University of Michigan function. In 1994, his football uniform number (48) was retired. *(Ford Library)*

No moniker could save Nixon — only Ford's September 8 "full, free, and absolute pardon" for all federal crimes Nixon "committed or may have committed or taken part in" from 1969-74.

Some wished Nixon to admit guilt before a pardon. Others wanted him tried, or hung. The fury stung; Ford's ratings plunged. Thus began a season of miscue and grisly luck. Out of the blue, the former All-American took to falling down stairs. Wife Betty had surgery to remove a cancerous right breast, and later discussed once-taboo abortion and marijuana. That fall, two people tried to kill Ford: Lynette Alice (Squeaky) Fromme and Sara Jane Moore, both pointing loaded pistols.

A January 1975 poll showed that only 18 percent of voters called themselves Republicans. On April 29, 1975, U.S. civilians left Saigon as Communist forces seized South Viet Nam. In August, Mrs. Ford told CBS' "60 Minutes" that she would not be shocked if teenage daughter Susan had an affair. Feminists likened her to Eleanor Roosevelt. The Right thought her the presidency's bane. Hearsay concerned Ford's Banquo's Ghost: Would Ronald Reagan challenge? Ford seemed Bill Mauldin's Sad-Sack beset by fate.

Thomas E. Dewey said, "Good government is good politics." Ford tried. He forced Rhodesia to abandon white minority rule, met with Leonid Brezhnev in Vladivostok, urged a global strategy to limit offensive nuclear arms, and signed the Helsinki Pact with the Soviet Union, Canada, and 32 European nations guaranteeing the integrity of national

Ford and Soviet leader Leonid Brezhnev at Vladivostok, November 23, 1974. The 38th president largely continued Richard Nixon's foreign policy of detente. *(Ford Library)*

The museum features the Oval Office as it existed in 1974-77. Its door was often open. "Yes, Congressmen will be welcome," Ford told them — "if you don't overdo it." *(Ford Library)*

boundaries. Khmer Rouge (Cambodian) forces captured a U.S. merchant ship, the *Mayaguez*, and refused to release it. Ford ordered an attack. Fifteen Marines were killed, and 50 wounded. Conservatives yawned.

Ford declared for president July 8, 1975. Reagan announced in November, and soon led among Republicans, 40 to 32 percent. On January 15, 1975, the incumbent had said, "The State of the Union is not good." It was better by 1976 — inflation down, faith renewed, America at peace — yet Ford was deemed tepid, dull — God place the

mark — too liberal! He opposed abortion, court-ordered busing, and gun control legislation, dropped detente from speeches, and vetoed bills — 66 in all. Nothing impressed the Right.

Ford won the nomination — 1,187 delegate votes to Reagan's 1,070 — but few now recalled the man of 1974 who rose at 5:15 A.M., made his own breakfast, read 12 newspapers, worked 18 hours daily, vowed "openness and candor," and seemed constitutionally unable to utter a nasty word.

Jimmy Carter led Ford by 33 points in August. It appeared a rout. Then, like a timer clicking, America reawoke to Ford as Jerry College to Nixon's — Carter's? — Uriah Heep.

DO YOU BELIEVE IN MIRACLES? Ford's is how he nearly won despite Watergate, the nightmare pardon, Bob Dole as vice-presidential nominee — "Democrats," he said in a TV debate, "have started all the wars in this century" — and claiming that Eastern Europe was not under Soviet domination. By Election Night, Ford's voice was spent. Betty read his concession speech.

Today, many vocal cords salute Ford's time. Was he just what the doctor ordered? Did his age end too soon because we dwarfed substance *v.* style? Say Ford, and you think of Nixon — to me, the first vote I cast in 1972. His opponent was George McGovern, whom I wrongly tabbed a symbol of Caligula's horse.

In 1979, I was sitting at National Airport in Washington for return to Upstate New York when — as Jack Paar would say, "I kid you not" — McGovern sat down next to me on the plane. He was to speak that night at Syracuse University. To my surprise, I found him likeable. Later, I would invoke that flight while saying, "Most of my friends are liberals."

Politics, I would learn, was not unlike, say, the law or sports. You could

fault the other side, and still allow for a real sense of friendship. But I should have known from 1974-77. Jerry Ford taught us that.

Gerald R. Ford Library. Richard Norton Smith, Director. 1000 Beal Avenue, Ann Arbor, Michigan 48109-2114. Phone: (313) 741-2218. Fax: (313) 741-2341.

Hours: Monday through Friday, 8:45 A.M. to 4:45 P.M. Open every day, except federal holidays. Saturday morning and occasional other hours are sometimes available by advance appointment. Free parking.

Gerald R. Ford Museum. Richard Norton Smith, Director. 303 Pearl Street, Northwest. Grand Rapids, Michigan 49504-5353. Phone: (616) 451-9263. Fax: (616) 451-9570. Web site: www.lbjlib.utexas.edu/ford.

Visitors have included: Presidents Carter, Reagan, and Bush. First Ladies Rosalynn Carter, Nancy Reagan, and Barbara Bush. Vice President Dan Quayle. British Prime Minister Lord James Callahan. Canadian President Pierre Trudeau. French President

★ ★ Windows on the White House ★ ★

Ford is the only president with a separate museum and library. The museum, shown here, hugs the Grand River in Grand Rapids. His library dots the University of Michigan. *(Above, JADEL. Below, Ford Library)*

Giscard D'estang. German President Helmut Schmidt. Mexican President Jose Lopez Portillo. Supreme Court Justice Clarence Thomas. Senator Bob Dole. Speaker of the House Tip O'Neill. Cabinet Secretaries James Baker, Dick Cheney, Carla Hills, Henry Kissinger, Lawrence O'Brien, and William Simon. Federal Reserve Chairman Alan Greenspan. General Colin Powell. Actors Chevy Chase and Bob Hope. Humorists Art Buchwald and Mark Russell.

Hours: Monday through Saturday, 9 A.M. to 4:45 P.M. Sunday, noon to 4:45 P.M. Open every day, except New Year's Day, Thanksgiving, and Christmas. Admission: Children age 15 years and under and school groups, free. Age 16 years and older, $2. Seniors age 55 and over, $1.50. Group tours are urged to make arrangements prior to visit. Free parking. Museum gift shop is open during regular hours.

★ ★ JERRY, BE GOOD ★ ★

The Ford Museum traces its adopted son from childhood to the present. The lobby features an Everett R. Kinstler portrait and 11 and 1/2-foot in diameter limestone presidential seal. *(Ford Library)*

SOME ROTARIAN! LEAVE IT TO Gerald Rudolph Ford to croon the fanfare of the (Un)Common Man. He was the first No. One not elected to the presidency or vice presidency. His post-presidency links biography — *A Time to Heal* — and specialty: the sole ex-president with a library and museum in different sites — Ann Arbor and Grand Rapids, respectively — his alma mater and boyhood home.

Ford's library buoys the University of Michigan. His museum, on a river in Grand Rapids, hails the greenery of the John Ford / "It's a Wonderful Life"/ made-in-USA small town. "Ford wanted it that way," said museum curator James Kratsas. "An All-American at Michigan, and local boy made good." Frank Merriwell, or Chip Hilton? Then and now, both co-exist in Ford.

"On the night he learned that he was likely to be the next President," Ronald Reagan said September 18, 1981, while dedicating Ford's museum, "he and Betty recited a favorite prayer from the book of Proverbs: 'Trust in the Lord with all thine heart; and lean not unto thine own understanding. In all thy ways acknowledge him, and he shall direct thy paths.'"

★ ★ WINDOWS ON THE WHITE HOUSE ★ ★

The library's begins with more than 20 million pages of papers and half a million audiovisual records. It turns to an automated database of about 50,000 index folder titles, zigs to congressional, veep, and presidential papers of Ford and his White House staff, and zags to issues from trade policy to sex discrimination to campaign media strategy and oceanic resources.

One hundred and thirty miles apart, the library and museum forge one institution. The library bulges with nine semi-trailer trucks of Ford papers shipped to Ann Arbor in 1977. Present are related collections about his, and others, times

— e.g. 1994 released material about 1969-75 backchannel communication between the White House and ambassador to Saigon that Ambassador Graham Martin took from the U.S. Embassy during its evacuation.

The files include Secretary of State Henry Kissinger's secret talks in Paris with Le Duc Tho of North Vietnam, and effect Watergate had on Viet Nam policy during Richard Nixon's second term. Cabinet meeting notes show Kissinger's spleen toward Congress: "This is the first time that American domestic reactions ... have impacted seriously on the action of a foreign government ... The

The museum interior upon its September 1981 opening. Pictured are exhibits which etch Ford's peregrination from Michigan via Yale to the Congress and vice presidency. *(Ford Library)*

Gerald Ford, in colonial garb, centers the museum's Bicentennial section. Said Ford on July 7, 1976: "Something wonderful happened to America this past weekend." *(Ford Library)*

most vocal critics during this period have been those people who got us into Indochina originally."

Kissinger was disgusted. In Ann Arbor, scholars are enriched.

PRESIDENT FORD HEALED "AMERica because he understood the adventure of America," said Reagan, "her way of governing, her people, and the source of her strength as a nation."

In 1994, the library marked Ford's 20th anniversary swearing-in with temporary exhibits. Visitors saw a 12-minute overview of the five days from Nixon's resignation to Ford's first address to Congress. "Gerald R. Ford Becomes Presi-

dent" mixed poster-sized photos and documents including Nixon's letter of resignation, highlights from Ford's inaugural speech, and a copy of the president's first daily diary — August 9, 1974.

The library leaves you with a grasp of what Ford was like. First, the jock. At Michigan, he lettered three years, helped win national titles in 1932-33, and was 1934 Most Valuable Player. An exhibit hails the conqueror via footballs, programs, recruiting letters, trophies, and photos from the '34 Michigan-Michigan State game. On October 8, 1994, the maize and blue retired Ford's number — 48 — before more than 102,000 fans.

Next, see how Ford loved the presidency, deeply and personally. A guest notes the still-photo coverage of Ford's daybook as president by David Kennerly, a photojournalist whom Ford met as vice president, and four other photographers. Available, too, are network news videotape, White House Communications Agency (WHCA) audiotape, and 16-millimeter color films shot by the Naval Photographic Center.

Ford never thought his job exquisite agony. "He hadn't sought, didn't expect to get it," said library director Richard Norton Smith. "He had told Mrs. Ford that they were going back to Grand Rapids when his House term ended [1975]. Instead, he became President through cir-

cumstance — and as unique as that was the fact that he never changed. He was one man assuming the Presidency. He was the same upon leaving it."

Many will endure Dante to possess the Oval Office. Once there, Ford aimed to keep it. Watch 1976 primary and general election Ford campaign ads, the 30-minute biography aired election eve, and spots from the campaigns of Reagan, Jimmy Carter, and others. Then, study Ford's response upon the White House's loss — and library conferences that show his faith in democracy.

"There are no soldiers marching except in the Inaugural Parade," Ford said in 1977 upon the changing of the guard. "No public demonstrations except for

For Gerald Ford, 1976 was bittersweet. On one hand, the Bicentennial. On the other, the Ford-Bob Dole ticket lost one of the closest elections in presidential history. *(Ford Library)*

some of the dancers at the Inaugural Ball. The opposition party doesn't go underground, but goes on functioning; and a vigilant press goes right on proving and publishing our faults and our follies."

Silently, Ford brooked loss to Carter, but stayed above ground. Ibid, his museum, which functions, said Smith, as "a nice building, [at a] wonderful location, which we're making nicer. Our exhibits were too flat, traditional. We're radically reworking them to make the visitor a participant, not spectator. We want to put this Presidency in the context of its time. For instance, we'll tell the story of how America's military buildup had its genesis in the Ford administration."

The $4 million reworking opened April 17, 1997. Unchanged is how the triangular, two-story museum with east wall of glass mirrors a panorama of the Grand River and Grand Rapids. Like the library, it shows a man comfortable in the presidency, and with himself.

FORD SEEMED TO SENSE THIS AT the 1981 dedication. "The finest tribute of all," he said, "will be to see the Gerald R. Ford Museum … living and growing and constructive" — an amalgam, among other things, of exhibit, text, and memory.

Each July 14, the museum celebrates Ford's birthday with cake for the first 500 visitors, and free admission all day. Also permanent are documents, graphics, video, and slide on the administration at apogee — the Helsinki Accords, or America's Bicentennial. Fixed in time is the Oval Office as it was in Ford's term in office. Luminous are the great French windows, thick carpet, fireplace, and still.

Enjoy Ford, as legislator: "How Laws are Made" yokes a cartooned wall of the process and multi-screen show of slides from nearly 100 photographers. Betty's husband: The "First Ladies' [Original] Gowns" exhibit salutes Mrs. Ford, Nancy Reagan, Barbara Bush, and Hillary Clinton, aided by photos and accessories. Chief Executive: presents include Royal Copenhagen China from Denmark from Heads of State, foreign leaders, and the American people. Finally, Ford, as minister of talent.

"He's proud of how his presidency was the training ground for a generation of leaders," said Smith. "George Bush, Henry Kissinger, Bill Simon, Alan Greenspan, Brent Scowcroft, Dick Cheney, Don Rumsfeld, Carla Hills. He surrounded himself with top-flight people. Visitors are impressed when they learn it, and with Ford's background. Eagle Scout. Adopted. World War II. Came up through Congress. Had the presidency thrust upon him. It resonates."

What resonates are exhibits like a

tiered-by-floor White House model, photo of Bob Hope viewing Bicentennial gifts from U.S. citizens, or "Great Decisions" lecture series. Said Ford: "They convey the texture and substance of this nation's experiment in self-government." Temporary exhibits pique interest in Political Americana, presidential cartoons and caricature, and "Quilts: A Bicentennial Celebration," of handmade quilts from across the USA.

Ford was lampooned as president, but took it well. In 1986, the museum conference, "Humor and the Presidency," boasted columnists, politicians, three Pulitzer cartoonists, and comics Chevy Chase and Art Buchwald. Another conference was organized by Mrs. Ford: "Modern First Ladies: Private Lives and Public Duties." Rosalynn Carter, the two Johnson daughters, and Susan Ford Vance recalled the White House fishbowl.

"You're not flown in from outer space to fulfill the special job," said Betty. "We bleed red blood. We cry real tears."

TEARS SHROUD THE VIET NAM Veterans Memorial in Washington, D.C. Dedicated on Veterans Day, 1982, it bears the name of casualties, dead, and missing. More than 25,000 mementoes have been left at the Wall since its groundbreaking — the first, a Purple Heart flung into wet cement.

A 1995-96 exhibit — "A Place of Tribute" — brought many artifacts and perhaps catharsis 700 miles to the north and west. Letter, poem, and object etched heartbreak — and heart-felt love — for the then-58,183 names engraved on the black granite wall.

"The Viet Nam exhibit crystalized Ford's duality," said James Kratsas. "On the minus side, Saigon's fall. The plus — summits with European leaders, Soviet detente, and a fidelity to trust. What a difference from the caricature of 'Saturday Night Live.' Maybe people didn't realize that in 1976. They do now."

A change of 11,000 votes, in different states, on November 2, 1976, would have re-elected No. 48. Did Nixon's pardon preclude victory? Would Ford grant it again? "I could not have conducted government," he said, "if this hadn't been resolved."

Many disagreed with Ford then. Few do, now. In Ann Arbor, and Grand Rapids, the time for healing seems complete.

★ ★ ★

Dedication excerpts, September 18, 1981.

"The first time he and I encountered each other was in Michigan. Well, it wasn't exactly an encounter, and we certainly didn't have any awareness of each

In a sense, Ford never left Grand Rapids. Exhibits recall his 1948 entree into politics. By then, "I had pretty well formed the … philosophy I've maintained ever since." *(Ford Library)*

other. I was a young sports announcer for station WHO in Des Moines, Iowa. I was broadcasting an Iowa-Michigan game. The center on that Michigan team was a fellow named Jerry Ford. Candor and a decent regard for history force me to admit that was about 47 years ago, and Michigan won." — Ronald Reagan

"To put it simply, we must decide whether we shall continue in the direction of recent years — the path toward bigger government, higher taxes, and higher inflation — or whether we shall now take a new direction, bringing to a halt the momentous growth of government, restoring our prosperity, and al-

lowing each of you a greater voice in your own future." — Gerald Ford

"Today many of us in public life, from this country and others, have come here to speak words of tribute to Gerald Ford. The millions of Americans who will soon hear or read these words will not long remember them, but we can be sure that in their minds and hearts there will be a flash of recognition and a swell of gratitude, feelings that if put into words would result in a simple statement by their countrymen about Gerald Ford: He was a good President who led us well, a good man who sought to serve others." — Ronald Reagan

To thrive, libraries and museums must remain contemporary. In 1996, the Ford Museum staged a straw poll. It evoked Truman against Dewey — or was it Ford *v.* Carter? *(Ford Library)*

"In the space of two centuries, we have not been able to right every wrong, to correct every injustice, to reach every worthy goal. But for 200 years we have tried and we will continue to strive to make the lives of individual men and women in this country and on this Earth better lives — more hopeful and happy, more prosperous and peaceful, more fulfilling, and more free. This is our common dedication, and it will be our common glory as we enter the third century of the American adventure."
— Gerald Ford

★ ★ ★

Library Directions: From the North (Flint), take Michigan Highway 23 south. Exit west on Geddes Road, which becomes Fuller Road. Take Beale Avenue north to the Ford Library. From the East (Detroit), take Interstate 94 west. Go north on Highway 23. Exit west on Geddes Road. Take Beale Avenue north to the library. From the South (Toledo), take 23 north to Geddes exit. Go west to Beale, then north to the library. From the West (Jackson), take

I-94 east. Go north on Highway 23, then west on Geddes Road. Exit Beale Avenue north to the library.

Museum Directions: From the North (Cadillac), go south on Michigan Highway 131. Exit east on Pearl Street and follow signs to the Ford Museum. From the East (Lansing), take Interstate 196 (Gerald R. Ford Freeway) west. Exit south on Ottawa Street. Proceed west on Pearl Street to the museum. From the South (Kalamazoo), go north on Highway 131. Exit east on Pearl Street and proceed to the museum. From the West (Holland), take I-196 east. Exit south on Highway 131. Go east on Pearl Street to the museum.

Taking the oath of office, August 9, 1974. "Our Constitution works," Ford observed. "Our great Republic is a government of laws and not men. Here, the people rule." *(Wide World Photos)*

Chapter 14

Deacon
Jimmy Carter Library

James Reston called Jimmy Carter's "The story of the small-town man [in his case, a peanut farmer from Plains, Georgia] who dreams of becoming president, and who by hard work and against incredible odds achieves his ambition." Carter came out of nowhere to win the presidency. He said he would earn our trust, and to many he did. Yet his administration is deemed by some a failure. Was that his fault, or theirs?

What endures are complex waves of imagery. The pastor/politician who vowed to make government good and full of love. The master of detail who weighed the forest against the trees. The softball-playing Georgian whose staff flaunted hardball. What are we to make of Carter's piety, ice blue eyes, and soft and easy smile?

Look homeward, angel: Carter's quandary stemmed from squaring Babylon on the Potomac with Plains' small shops, red clay, and witching power. His town prized faith, feeling, and fidelity to honor. The capital's ruling class shared biases and deities: Chanel, Armani, networking and business cards, debating who's up and down.

Plains drank beer, not Perrier; confused the rap singer Hammer with Armand Hammer; and regarded its favorite Guy as Lombardo. Washington, D.C.'s permanent aristoi consisted, variously, of lawyers, lobbyists, trendies, preppies, and self-dubbed tastemakers. To Carter, they were SSBPs — Self-Styled Better People — with depth akin to a 30-second ad.

Plains scent of Roy Acuff. Washington reeked of Oscar Wilde. Carter didn't drink. Too bad. He might have toasted trouble in the brewing. Ying and yang. Round holes and oblong pegs. Washington is where he worked. Plains is what he loved.

Jimmy Carter, coatless, in a common pose. "Carter's story is the stuff of retelling," the author writes. "Lyrically, indelibly — it belongs to us all." *(Carter Library)*

"JIMMY WAS ALWAYS THE SMART-est of the class," said a public school-mate. Carter left Plains for the Naval Academy, volunteered for submarine duty, and joined an elite group of officers on the first nuclear-powered submarines. His boss was Captain Hyman Rickover. Wrote the seaman: "He had a [more] profound influence on my life than any-one except my own parents."

In 1953, his father died of cancer, and Carter returned to Plains to manage the family business. Next, politics. He was elected to the 1963-67 Georgia Sen-ate, lost for governor in 1966, and won in 1970. His chief foe was the Georgia Constitution: It forbade re-election.

If law closed doors, Carter could open others. In September 1973, his mother, Miss Lillian, asked what he in-tended to do.

"I'm going to run for President."
President of what?

"Momma, I'm going to run for President of the United States, and I'm going to win." What a quipster! thought Miss Lillian. Her son wasn't joking.

Carter announced in December 1974, and forever changed the web of nomination. His guerrilla campaign still evokes '40s Mao v. Chiang Kai-shek. His bayonets were surprise and satura-tion. He virtually lived in Iowa, the first caucus to elect delegates to the 1976 Democratic Convention, and then the

Carter took office vowing to dismantle doors between the president and body politic. To a large degree he did. *(Carter Library)*

New Hampshire Primary. A reporter wrote: "The message was primarily Jimmy Carter, a man of warmth and de-cency. It won him the nomination."

Populism clung to Carter like scan-dal to U.S. Grant. He said grace, wore blue jeans, and carried his own bags. The Democratic Party was thought elit-ist, secular, and wastrel. Carter was a born-again, businessman, post-Watergate moralist. How antipodal to the hated Nixon! What a vision must exist in Carter's retaking the Solid South: Democrats' ticket back to power.

Tag it discount; he beat Gerald Ford by only 297-240 electoral votes. Mandate, or boydate? Carter said the former, and blitzed Capitol Hill. His first major act was to pardon nearly 10,000 Viet Nam draft evaders. He created two new federal agencies, and said America would return the Canal to Panama by the year 2000. Proposed: tax reform, electoral reform, and a new welfare system. Affirmed: the energy crisis as "the moral equivalent of war." Too much, too soon? Not to Carter, who challenged Congress: Match my good will with your good policy.

Key was popularity. Voters had to tell the Hill to let the Outsider lead. In turn, popularity rested on how the prestige press shaped his image. Carter's problem was a D.C. culture shaped by the elite, not middle, class. Carter didn't fit. He was bright, twitted Georgetown, but was he smart? He never attended boarding school, skied in Aspen, or vacationed in Belize. SSBPs never got how Carter solved moral dilemma in the Bible. Carter never grasped why to Official Washington, dilemma meant whether to eat at Dominique's or The Palm.

On Inaugural Day, Carter had walked down Pennsylvania Avenue. Later, he banned "Hail to the Chief," gave fireside chats in a sweater, and held picnics on the White House lawn. How could Congress spurn a man who canceled chauffeur service, asked his staff not to live in sin, and that first year held more press conferences, saw more visitors, and talked to the people more than any president since FDR? Quickly, as it happened.

In a year, Carter's popularity plunged from 75 to 56 percent. It was inexorable, and perhaps inevitable. To Washington, he was not Our Guy.

IN HIS INAUGURAL, CARTER quoted a high school teacher, Miss Julia Coleman: "We must adjust to changing times and still hold to unchanging principles." To Carter, principle meant peace.

Was he too noble for the job? At certain moments Utopia didn't hurt. Carter yanked troops from Korea, signed a nuclear non-proliferation pact with the U.S.S.R. and 13 other nations, and normalized relations with China after 30 years of quarantine. Add the high sky of September 1978: For 13 days, Carter wooed Israeli Prime Minister Menachem Begin and Egyptian President Anwar Sadat at Camp David. Only Nixon could go to China. Only this "I am a deeply religious man" could nudge Begin and Sadat toward ending the Egypt-Israeli conflict.

Later, Carter said, "It [the presidency] is much more complex than I anticipated." It didn't seem so at the time. Then, in early 1979, a gas shortage occurred after Iran cut America's flow of oil. Its offspring were long lines, high prices, and unemployment. "You couldn't go into a store with a 10-dollar bill," said economist Sylvia Porter, "and come out with much of a bag of groceries." At Camp David, Carter queried aides, cabinet members, governors, and solons: Where had the dream gone wrong? He emerged to give a talk — to Ted Kennedy, the "Malaise" speech — which touted energy self-sufficiency, scored a "crisis of the spirit," and sought to lift his approval rating — 17 percent.

Carter's inaugural had vowed a season in the sun. His presidency now wilted in the rain. In 1977, he said, "We have an inordinate fear of Communism." In late 1979, the Soviets invaded Afghanistan. Carter conceded shock, embargoed sales of grain and technology, and boycotted Moscow's 1980 Summer Olympics. At the same time, he let the exiled Shah of Iran enter the U.S. for medical treatment.

On November 4, 1979, forces of Islamic leader Ayatollah Khomeini seized 63 Americans at the Embassy in Teheran. Six months later, eight soldiers died trying to rescue hostages still in the Embassy. Forget Inchon, or Bastogne.

Teddy Roosevelt's "big stick" seemed a sling-shot. Abroad — at home — people winced, not wept. U.S. power had flown the cage.

CARTER BEGAN CALLING THE presidency too big for any man. Many thought that a dog that wouldn't hunt. Dogging him were inflation's 15 percent and interest rates at 20. Said Ronald Reagan: "Are you better off than you were four years ago?" Carter wasn't. In 1980, he got 49 electoral votes to Reagan's 489 — the first incumbent president since Hoover to lose.

Peggy Lee sang, "Is that all there is?" With Carter, no. He endured life's darkest pitch to find dignity in survival — and survival in hope. He built homes for Habitat for Humanity, and became an ambassador without portfolio to Haiti, Korea, and the Middle East. Some dubbed Carter a free-lancer. More came to judge him — and his world-view of curious tenderness — with emotion akin to growing respect.

The Ghosts of the Carter Age — his peanut farm, and crooked smile. Killer rabbit. "Lust in my heart." Miss Lillian, daughter Amy, wife Rosalynn, and brother Billy — carry us to years when a majority worried that things were running out. In response, Carter spent his post-presidency seeking what he thought would sustain the pastiche of time — renewal, not memory.

This oil on canvas portrait, from the United Mexican States, etches the president who said, "I am an American and a southerner — also, a husband, father, and businessman." *(Carter Library)*

Jimmy Carter Library. Atlanta, Georgia. The scent of populist pastor/politician pervades each of the Carter Center's five pavilions, including the library. *(Carter Library)*

He found it in Plains' — not the capital's — priorities. Service. Help the needy. Tend a wound. Lend a hand. In 1975, Carter wrote his biography, *Why Not the Best?* Goodness had been his alpha, then. His omega — America's shy, tardy gratitude — had finally come again.

Jimmy Carter Library. Dr. Donald B. Schewe, Director. 441 Freedom Parkway and One Copenhill Avenue, Northeast. Atlanta, Georgia 30307-1406. Phone: (404) 331-3942. Fax: (404) 703-2215. Web sites: (Carter Center) http://www. emory.edu/cartercenter/homepage.html. (National Archives) http://www.nara.gov or http://gopher. nara.gov:70/l/inform/library/carter. (Sunsite) http://sunsite://unc.edu/lia/president/carter.html.

Visitors have included: Presidents Ford, Reagan, and Bush. First Ladies Betty Ford, Nancy Reagan, and Barbara Bush. Secretary of State Warren Christopher. Chief Justice Warren Burger. King Hussein and Queen Noor of Jordan. Archbishop Desmond Tutu. Atlanta Mayor Andrew Young. Historian John Kenneth Galbraith. Actors Richard Dreyfus and Jane Fonda.

Hours: Monday through Saturday, 9 A.M. to 4:45 P.M. Sunday, noon to 4:45 P.M. Open every day, except New Year's Day, Thanksgiving, and Christmas. Admission: Children under 16 free. Seniors 55 and over, $4. Others, $6. Group tours are urged to make arrangements prior to visit. Call (404) 331-3942. Free parking. Library gift shop is open during regular hours.

★ ★ ★

OXYMORON DESCRIBES THE "TYPI-cal" presidential library. FDR's slate roof and local fieldstone might not work in Southern California. Envision LBJ's behemoth in Independence. You can't; Truman oozed humility. Transplant the sprawling Reagan Library to West Branch, Iowa. The swap doesn't fit in intellectual luggage. Hoover, for one thing, was a man of understatement.

Libraries heed Polonius: "To thine own self be true." Film festivals buoy Grand Rapids, but not Fremont. In Yorba Linda, the gift shop sells T-shirts of Nixon meeting Elvis Presley. "I don't think we

Carter hoped to build a library beyond books and stills. His center addresses issues that he faced as president — e.g. poverty, disease, and human rights. *(Carter Library)*

A foyer epigraph reads: "I want the … Center to be a great resource for the people of … the world and an expression of my gratitude for having been able to serve." — Jimmy Carter *(Carter Library)*

sell anything you would describe as silly," remarks Kennedy curator Frank Rigg. Ike's knotty pine recalls the 1950s. Push-button exhibits invoke engineer-president Jimmy Carter's interest in the here and high-tech.

Fit at birth counts as well. The Presidential Libraries Act requires a library to acquire land, raise money, and give buildings and papers to the National Archives. Uniformity then stops. Each building's core and place reflect its

subject. Leaving office, for instance, the 39th president's decision about his papers already had been made.

In 1977, Carter vowed to build his library "somewhere in Georgia." After Reagan's election, he foresaw better days by moving his papers there and writing his memoirs. In 1981, Carter chose a site, 176 miles from Plains, that belonged to the state's Department of Transportation. The Carter Foundation then began talks to secure title, and land.

"In dedicating this Center today," Reagan said five years later, "I want to express ... that this celebration is in a sense a celebration of the South — the new South that Jimmy Carter helped to build." Aptly, the library rose where the Old South died — high, on a ridge, where General Sherman headquartered during the Battle of Atlanta. Yankee, schmankee. Carter liked it. It was already an old friend.

In 1969, the land had been condemned to build an interstate highway spur between downtown Atlanta and Stone Mountain. The road never happened; civic opposition led then-Governor Carter to halt construction. Oh, irony! In 1982, Carter asked the state DOT to build an access road — whereupon many of the same civic groups sued the "Presidential Parkway."

Carter won, and the library opened October 1, 1986. He would never lie to you: It was a delicious, if belated, twist.

ALL PRESIDENTS ARE AWARE OF age. At 45, John Kennedy hosted a stag dinner at 1600 Pennsylvania Avenue for distinguished Harvard alumni. Most were a generation or two older. "It is difficult to welcome you to the White House," he told them, "because at least two-thirds of you have attended more stag dinners here than I have."

Carter was conscious, too — at 56,

younger than most ex-presidents on leaving office. His goal: a full and vivid life. A mere library might not fit the bill. What might was a continuum of circular buildings around a man-made lake that housed programs dedicated to peace, human rights, democracy, and development, and aimed at poverty, hunger, and disease.

The Carter Center staffs a library and museum, offices of the Task Force for Child Survival, Global 2000 Inc., Carter Center of Emory University, and the Carter-Menil Human Rights Foundation. Four of the five pavilions house offices for the Carters and the center programs, affiliated with Emory University. The Carter Library occupies Pavilion V.

"People tour the center," said library director Dr. Donald Schewe, "and then we hear their thoughts. We get from Republicans, 'Gee, I didn't know he did all this.' Or from Democrats, 'You didn't have enough on Camp David, say, or campaign reform.' You don't hear good things, but criticism from both sides. Maybe that's good. I think it means we're fair."

Bipartisanship thrives — also, interior design — amid concrete, granite, and glass, accented by bronze and mahogany, that link pieces of the center jigsaw. Enter through a foyer, reached through a covered walkway, that includes a thermal-finished granite marker with the presidential seal. To the left lies a the-atre. A nearby commons room hosts de-bate among scholars — and exhibits, among laity.

"Perspective is what we want. Camp David was not a friendly confab," Schewe said. "It was hammer and tong, back and forth. At any point in 13 days the whole thing could have gone 'kablooey.'" Perspective clings. "We're not talking to a hostile audience. You don't get a universe of Gingrich Re-publicans coming here, or liberal Demo-crats going to the Reagan Library."

The incongruity is that Carter's mu-seum and theatre-in-the round video air themes — human rights, the environ-ment, nuclear proliferation, a non-iso-lated China — that vibrate even with non-Carter voters. So, darkly, does the Iranian hostage crisis.

All dot a museum with closed-circuit TV — punch buttons, and get Carter's "personal" answers — that sketch his life, family history, and the American presidency.

"[THE PRESIDENCY] IS AN OFFICE held in solitary confinement," Warren Christopher said, dedicating the library.

As president, Carter invented the town meeting. This exhibit recalls how he met people across the U.S. to answer questions and find what was on their minds. *(Carter Library)*

The Middle East has known rancor since before the Scriptures. It took a true believer and student of the Bible to turn swords into plowshares and spears into pruning hooks. *(Carter Library)*

"A President faces monumental duties with a sense of power and powerlessness, exhilaration and frustration, surrounded by people but inevitably lonely." Alone, Carter fixed on the goodness he perceived in America. You feel natural asking the personal — "Was your White House the first to serve grits?" — or historic. "Why did you choose to go to Camp David with Begin and Sadat?"

"Town Hall" is a favorite interactive video display. Also popular are Americans' homemade gifts, a formal White House dinner setting, video-taped events in the family quarters, and exhibits like the Carters' July 7, 1946 wedding day photo — oil on canvas portrait, from the United Mexican States — and gold evening purse with diamonds, rubies, and green onyx, the Kingdom of Morocco.

Carter was wrongly judged a non-politician. He excelled, shrewdly and personally. It shows in the posters, "Jimmy Carter for President" and "A New Spirit. A New Commitment. A New America. President Jimmy Carter." The impression grows via black and white photos of Carter shoveling peanuts;

on a motorcycle; in his ensign's uniform with his new bride at his side; and an old campaign poster that reads, "Hello. My name is Jimmy Carter. I'm running for President."

He ran partly to redeem his 1971 Georgia Inaugural Address: "I say to you quite frankly that the time for racial discrimination is over ... No poor, rural, weak, or black person should ever again have to bear the additional burden of being deprived of the opportunity for an education, a job, or simple justice." As president, Carter's burden draped the

Oval Office, replicated here to look like his White House.

The fireplace, furniture, rug, architecture, window decor, wallpaper, and George Washington painting recall 1977-81. Through the window, back-lit transparencies mirror the Potomac, not Plains. "In the Oval Office, the exterior view is of Washington," said Carter. "Then go outside and you're back in Georgia." It is, you suspect, a trade he is glad to make.

"THE SINGLE MOST POPULAR EX-

TIME once said that "Carter's distance from the Oval Office has been his strength, and with luck and skill could be his genius." The library's Oval Office. *(Carter Library)*

hibit is the Oval Office," said Schewe. "The most common question is whether it is full-scale. The most frequent comment is that he's the greatest former president we've had. Each exhibit is linked with something particular — and if it achieves that, we hope it speaks to people individually."

The library speaks to scholars, with 27 million pages of Carter's personal and public papers. Stored and catalogued are letters, appointment books, legislative records, and signed treaties like the Egypt-Israeli and Panama Canal accords. Upstairs are the archivists' offices, a reading room, vaults, and storage facilities. They house about 1.5 million photos (FDR had less than 100,000) and several thousand hours of videotape (unknown at FDR's death in 1945).

Many detail Carter the humanitarian. "When Jimmy Carter was born on this date in 1924, many southerners knew only poverty, and millions lived lives that were separate and unequal because of the color of their skin," said Reagan in 1986. Others salute the peacemaker. The center has sponsored high-level talks on the Middle East, Arms Control, Conflict Resolution, the Latin American Debt Crisis, and Global Health.

"Going through the Jimmy Carter Library just now and admiring the many photographs and films," Reagan added, "it struck me that perhaps the central gift that this center will give to the Nation is a story — a story of one man's life, a story that is distinctively American."

In Atlanta, your mind sees him working at his desk, repairing to a quiet site, or studying in his office hideaway. Carter's story is the stuff of retelling. Lyrically, indelibly — it belongs to us all.

Dedication excerpts, October 1, 1986.

"Time and again throughout his life, at moments great and small, President Carter has turned to prayer. When he learned that John Kennedy had been assassinated, Jimmy Carter knelt outside the farm warehouse in prayer. When he became President himself, it was prayer that sustained him. He knew that ... as Lincoln put it, the burdens of the highest office in the land would be intolerable without the help of the Almighty. And I wouldn't be surprised to learn that when he got up this morning President Carter said a prayer of thanks for all that would happen this day." — Ronald Reagan

"I listened to your [Reagan's] speech with great attention. I don't think I have ever heard one that was more generous and more gracious and more thoughtful. And if you'll permit me to inject a political note, into an otherwise bi-partisan occasion, as I listened to you speak a few minutes ago, I understood more clearly

than I ever have in my life, why you won in November 1980 and I lost." — Jimmy Carter

"History may longest remember President Carter as a global champion of human rights. Through this center, he remains at the side of all who are made to suffer for their station, color, or belief." — Warren Christopher

"This is indeed a great day for higher education in this whole region ... The Carter Center is dedicated to seek in George Eliot's fine phrase, 'To influence the standards of mankind, for generations yet to come.' With President Carter, in our work and in our programs, we share that vision in that hope." — Emory University President James T. Laney

★ ★ ★

Directions: From the South, take Interstate-75/85 North to Exit 96A (Boulevard/Glen Iris) and turn left at dead end. Turn right at North Highland Avenue, go 1/2 mile to Cleburne Avenue, and turn left into the Carter Library parking lot. From the West, take I-20 east to the Moreland Avenue (Route 23) exit. Go north on Moreland to Freedom Parkway. Turn left and follow signs to the library. From the North, take I-75/85 south to Exit 100 (North Avenue) and turn left. At North Highland, turn right. Go one block to Cleburne Avenue, and turn right into the lot. From the East, take Briarcliff Road to Ponce de Leon Avenue and turn right. Go one block to North Highland and turn left. Go to Cleburne Avenue and turn right into the library.

Flags at the entrance salute what a writer termed "a liberal, moderate, conservative, compassionate, ruthless, soft, tough" complex president and superb ex-president. *(Carter Library)*

CHAPTER 15

THE GIPPER
RONALD REAGAN LIBRARY
AND MUSEUM

(Ronald Reagan Library and Museum.)

HIS AUTOBIOGRAPHY WAS *An American Life*. His life bespoke an American Original. His heart, he wrote, "is a ham loaf." As president, it warmed the nation's plate. Ronald Reagan's sense of humor made him unusual in Washington: a politician who was funny on purpose. He was also a prophet in his time.

Reagan was a political prophet —

foreboding America's trek toward conservatism. Next, a Mayberry prophet — presaging its revolt against elites. His wife, Nancy, said, "Politics can be vicious. Ronnie is strong and gentle." Reagan evoked the heartland of Jimmy Stewart — its address, he said, "hopeful, big-hearted, idealistic, daring, decent, and fair."

Think of whistlestops from Dixon

In his 70s, the Gipper at Camp David — since FDR, a presidential retreat. *(Reagan Library)*

Across 1981-89, millions forgot to check mythy faith at the door. Their trust rose from flag-waving, Reagan's charm, supply-side economics, America's remembered and/or reinvented past, and concern for its New Jerusalem. On Inauguration Day 1981, clouds on a gloomy morn yielded as the national prophet rose to speak.

Harbinger, or Irish luck? Who says that one voids the other?

REAGAN HOPED TO SPUR OPPORtunity, not government, by spurning quantitative measurement — legislation now, and hang the content — a frenzy of activity for activity's sake. So he lowered taxes, assailed regulation, cut the rate of spending, and spun America's longest peacetime boom — its largest-ever deficit, too.

Reagan believed that the judiciary should interpret, not legislate. So he appointed judges not prone to social engineering. Was America divinely blessed? Reagan urged that voluntary prayer again grace public school. Did his agenda last? Is Don Knotts unforgettable as Barney Fife? Reagan's "smaller is better government — rebuild the military — the old ways are best" dominated the off-year Election of 1994.

A Gallup Poll that year asked Americans to rate the 1980s. By three to one, they felt well, not ill. Reagan took the oath as taxes had quadrupled in 15 years,

and Tampico to Eureka College and WHO Radio, Des Moines. Reagan sprang from the heart of America — culturally, and geographically. Not even a would-be assassin could best him. Shot in March 1981, he looked at doctors in the emergency room and said, "I hope you're all Republicans." Later, Reagan told Nancy, "Honey, I forgot to duck."

and personal savings were worst since 1951. By 1989, the private sector had spun more than 19 million new jobs. A president should keep us prosperous, strong abroad, and link resolve (say, tax reform, a freeze on federal hiring, and firing air traffic controllers) and geniality (ribbing age; "There you go again"; telling Tip O'Neill, "We're friends after 6 o'clock"). Reagan did.

Reagan talked of "winning one for the Gipper." The Gipper as global prophet helped win one for freedom's cup. He refilled the "Hollow Army," closed the "Window of Vulnerability," bore the Strategic Defense Initiative, and assigned Communism to history's dust bin. June 12, 1987, at Berlin's Brandenburg Gate: "Mr. Gorbachev, tear down this wall!"

Clark Clifford called Reagan "an amiable dunce." Jesse Jackson likened him to Judas Iscariot. To O'Neill, he was "ignorant" — a "sin that he is President." Reagan, on the other hand, discerned how 1977-81 made us feel that "the mausoleum was in our heart." (Robert Lowell, 1953) Curative was his defense buildup

The 40th president with Soviet leader Mikhail Gorbachev. In May 1988, Reagan carved the ultimate photo opportunity — strolling through Moscow's Red Square. *(Reagan Library)*

Cold moved the 1985 inaugural inside. Reagan takes the oath of office. *(Reagan Library)*

— $1 trillion in eight years. In 1980, a U.S. hostage rescue failed when four helicopters burned in the Iranian desert. By decade's end, the military was the institution that Gallup said inspired most respect, and would be trusted in a crisis.

Reagan saw what blinded Georgetown: Re. national defense, finishing second meant finishing last. In a reverse twist of fate, the Cold Warrior/ Evil Empire-baiter rebuilt America's strength — then, used it to spin the first

Strategic Arms Reduction Treaty — START 1 — and what George Bush called the New World Order.

Margaret Thatcher said that great leaders are summed up in a sentence. "I will sum up the achievements of President Reagan in a sentence, too. Ronald Reagan won the Cold War without firing a shot."

FOR ONCE, HISTORY IS NOT DEbatable. Reagan's parade of '80s hits fused Normandy and Libya and Grenada and Red Square. "We will negotiate for it [peace], sacrifice for it; we will not surrender for it now or never," read Reagan's first inaugural. More nod now than sensed so at the time.

Was he errant in detail, contradictory in ad-lib utterance, less telling in a press conference than stump speech? Yes/yet: No leader since Churchill so used Billy Graham's mantra: "Repeat, repeat, repeat." Reagan's

The Bible of Reagan's mother, used for the '85 swearing-in at the Capitol. *(Reagan Library)*

★ ★ THE GIPPER ★ ★

Speaking to U.S. troops at Camp Liberty Bell along Korea's demilitarized zone, November 1983. The Gipper returns to Notre Dame to give the 1981 Commencement speech. *(Reagan Library)*

— "Family, work, neighborhood, freedom, peace" — helped liberty unchain the world.

Custom called him a cowboy, or adventurer. Truth is more complex than their alarum or Reagan's nice-guy manner. The son of an alcoholic shoe salesman grew up in sober Sinclair Lewis towns. A fine actor, he became the Errol Flynn of the Bs. "I made quite a few movies where they didn't want them good — they wanted them Tuesday." Private — "Nancy and I don't show our souls" — the Gipper loved the mashed potato and lecture circuit. Later, the politician could kiss babies, wear funny hats, and glad-hand with the best.

Go figure. From, but never of, Hollywood, he remained what he termed "an old-fashioned square." He led a crusade — but as friend William Buckley said, was "too modest and fatalistic to be a crusader." His courtesy and likeability ("Little House on the Prairie" was Reagan's favorite TV show) foiled bids to paint him The Ghost of Goldwater Past. A final quirk: Fortune's Son reached the presidency at 69 only after a 1968 run against Nixon, near-miss '76 loss to Ford, and pummeling by the Eastern press.

Working on his 1982 State of the Union Address. Reagan's bent for rhetoric — polished from '30s radio to the White House — led to his moniker, "The Great Communicator." *(Reagan Library)*

Reagan expanded Nixon's coalition of farmers, small businessmen, blue-collars, union members, Catholics, and Southern Protestants. A writer defined his flock as "Main Street, and specifically, the people reviled in *Main Street* ... for whom citizenship has more to do with loyalty than with ideology." Reagan never fled his 1967 inaugural address as incoming California governor. "We have been told there are no simple answers to complex problems. Well, the truth is there are simple answers, just not easy ones."

Critics called him a hater. Again, fact cleaves. Reagan sought endlessly to grasp other points of view. One must provoke to arouse real anger.

How do you describe the typical Washington economic adviser? "He has a Phi Beta Kappa key on his watch chain — and no watch on the other end."

Once, he spied several unkempt protestors with "Make love, not war" signs. Reagan told the rally: "They don't look as if they're capable of doing either."

Wright Morris wrote of Norman Rockwell, "His special triumph is in the conviction his countrymen share that the mythical world he evokes exists." Parkbench Americanism tugged at Reagan's sleeve. Also, courage — stumping in '64 for hapless Goldwater, defending Nixon amid Watergate, or writing a 1994 open letter baring Alzheimer's disease. Like

Don Quixote, he lanced at windmills — except that the Gipper's often fell.

Weak after being shot, Reagan one day spilled water from the hospital sink. Entering the room, aides found him in the bathroom on hands and knees — trying to wipe up water so the nurse wouldn't get into trouble. How to forget such a man? Many haven't to this day.

ASKED WHOM HE MOST ADMIRED, Reagan often said, "The man from Galilee." Unmoved by fashion, he moved the unhip and unboutique. His America, and theirs — John Winthrop's "Shining City on a Hill" — scorned the view that the presidency was passe.

When Reagan's favorite president died in 1945, *The New York Times* wrote, "Men will thank God on their knees, a hundred years from now, that Franklin D. Roosevelt was in the White House." It may not take a hundred years to grasp how Reagan spurned fear, renewed his office, and freed America from hemorrhage.

Quoting Sophie Tucker — who, in turn, quoted Al Jolson — Reagan loved to say, "You ain't seen nothin' yet!" Did he mean America, or his administration?

Nancy Reagan, greeting children in a 1984 tour of Rainbow Bridge Township, Shanghai. "She is my rock," said her husband. "Each day matters because of her." *(Reagan Library)*

The Reagan Library and Museum. Simi Valley, California. "The presidency is an institution," said Reagan. "It was my privilege to be given temporary custody." *(Reagan Library)*

It was hard to distinguish in the 1980s. What is not is how he turned the winter of our discontent into a springtime of possibility.

Ronald Reagan Library and Museum. Mark Hunt, Director. 40 Presidential Drive, Simi Valley, California 93065-0666. Phone: (805) 522-8444. Fax: (805) 522-9621. Web site: http://sunsite.unc.edu/lia/president/pres.html.

Visitors have included: Presidents Nixon, Ford, Carter, and Bush. First Ladies Lady Bird Johnson, Pat Nixon, Betty Ford, Rosalynn Carter, and Barbara Bush. Vice President Dan Quayle. Lady Margaret Thatcher. Soviet President Mikhail Gorbachev, and wife Raisa. Canadian Prime Minister Brian Mulroney, and wife Misa. King Hussein of Jordan, and Queen Noor. Speaker of the House Newt Gingrich. Secretaries of State James Baker and George Schultz. General Colin Powell. Julie Nixon Eisenhower and Tricia Nixon Cox, Luci Johnson Turpin, Susan Ford Bales, Caroline Schlossberg and John Kennedy, Jr. Actors Charlton Heston, Bob Hope, Arnold Schwarzenegger, and Jimmy Stewart. Journalists Hugh Sidey and Helen Thomas. Entertainer Larry King.

Hours: Daily, 10 A.M. to 5 P.M. Open every day, except New Year's Day, Thanksgiving, and Christmas. Admission: Children age 15 years and under, free. Age 16 years and older, $4. Seniors age 62 and over, $2. Groups of 20 or more should make reservations by calling the Tour Desk, which is open 9 A.M. to noon, Monday through Friday. Free parking. Library gift shop is open during regular hours.

★ ★ ★

"[LIBRARY VISITORS] WILL OBserve an American president and a Soviet leader, sitting in a boathouse on the shore of Lake Geneva, striving to banish the nuclear nightmare from the dreams of all our children," said Ronald Reagan on dedication day.

"They will see tears of pride from the boys of Pointe Du Hoc. They will hear the thrusting engines of Challenger lifting off on a heart-breaking final mission ... They will catch the sinister crackle of a would-be assassin's weapon ... [affirming] my belief that whatever time remained to me was to be spent in service to the American people and in accord with the Lord's wishes."

Best wishes laureled November 4, 1991 — by dint of uncoincidence, the 11th anniversary of Reagan's election as president. On a hilltop near Simi Valley, about 35 miles northwest of Los Angeles,

The Reagan Library research room. Here lies much of the largest collection of presidential material of any library — 50 million pages, or 23,500 feet. *(Reagan Library)*

amid 100 acres of scrub-covered terrain, the 91,193-square-foot, $56.8 million Reagan Library and Museum opened on a stage behooving the Gipper of film.

Universal Studios designed the sound, platform, and lighting. The invitation-only audience linked Sacramento and Washington — 4,200 former aides, campaign junkies, Stagedoor Johnnies, and other admirers. The building, two-thirds of it underground, had a red tile roof, affected a Spanish mission, and brought Reagan home. Below were the rocky, dust-brown hills of Hollywood westerns: Reagan had climbed them as King of the Bs.

Name a more dazzling cast. As Sam Goldwyn said, "In two words — im-possible." For the first time in history, five United States presidents had gathered in one place — Nixon, Ford, Carter, Bush, and Reagan — and wives Pat, Betty, Rosalynn, Barbara, and the Lady in Red. Said Reagan: "I can't begin to describe what [Nancy] means to me except to say I can't imagine life without her." For those who still regarded him as actor, not politician, it was hard to imagine the day.

"From 1862 until Bush's '89 inauguration," said library director Mark Hunt, "there had never been more than three former presidents alive at the same time."

At Simi Valley, the Club of White House Families — Lady Bird Johnson, daughter Luci Johnson Turpin, Caroline Schlossberg, John Kennedy, Jr., and heirs of Franklin Roosevelt — tried to make up for lost time.

"WE FEW, WE HAPPY FEW," WROTE Shakespeare, "we band of brothers." On November 4, Commanders in Chief spoke one for the Gipper.

"[Reagan's defense buildup]," said Nixon, "made it possible for George Bush to implement his brilliant strategy for victory in the Gulf War."

Added Ford: "[Reagan] was able to articulate the highest hopes and deepest beliefs of the American people."

Observed Bush: "Here are four former presidents — [and] former first ladies — dedicated public servants — each part of the American story." The library's story wends like frames in flag-waving/cracker barrel/village green/ Capra celluloid.

It began, as Reagan said in 1991, in "Dixon, Illinois. [We] may have had little in material terms, but we were emotionally wealthy beyond imagination ... I grew up in a town where everyone cared about one another because everyone knew one another. Our neighbors were never embarrassed to kneel in prayer to their maker. Nor were they ever embarrassed to feel a lump in their throat when Old Glory passed by. No one in Dixon, Illinois, ever burned a flag. No one in Dixon would have tolerated it."

Reagan liked to quote Al Jolson and Sophie Tucker: "You ain't seen nothin' yet!" This exhibit recalls that, and other, moments, from his 1980 and '84 landslide victories. *(Reagan Library)*

Two thousand miles from Dixon, Reaganism — the message, and messenger — summoned that America's swelling sense of pride. Ground was broken November 21, 1988. Archives opened for research November 12, 1991. The central courtyard joins wings that hold about 50 million pages of documents, including records of the president and staff members, 1.5 million still photos, and more than 75,000 gifts. Other numbers: 550,000 feet of film, 25,000 video tapes, 26,000 sound recordings, 15,000 books, and 75,000 museum objects in 22,000 square feet of exhibit space. Each public photo and item was checked and approved by America's First Couple, 1981-89.

Exhibit areas include the Presidents Gallery, Early Years, Road to the Presidency, the World in 1980, Prosperity, Head of State Gifts, Peace and Freedom, Voices of Freedom, Legacy Video, Oval Office Replica, Life in the White House, First Lady's Gallery, and "Meet President Reagan" Interactive Video Theater. Wrote *The Washington Post*: "[Reagan] is depicted in all stages of his career as an earnest striver who followed his dreams, became disillusioned with the increasing power and reach of government, cut his Democratic moorings, became the two-term Republican Governor of California, and, then, as President, restored the faith of America in their country."

VISITORS PICK AND CHOOSE AT A library. Reagan's is no exception. Its odyssey links Hollywood gimcracks, a re-created White House State dinner, replica of the Oval Office, nuclear cruise missile killed by the Intermediate-Range Nuclear Force (INF) Treaty, declassified corrrespondence between signees Presidents Reagan and Mikhail Gorbachev, medal taken from a destroyed Soviet SS-120 missile, and piece of that ubiquitous Berlin Wall — 9-feet-5 inches tall, 3-feet-5 inches wide, and 6,338 pounds large — on the west terrace above the sea.

Carter told the dedication, "What bonds us together best of all is our common commitment to freedom." A library video —"Economic Recovery in the Reagan Years" — likens Reagan to another Democrat, Franklin Roosevelt. Other videos and wall scripts address Iran-Contra, including a "Peace and Freedom" foreign policy timeline — Reagan's March 30, 1981 shooting. As a movie star, Reagan played the boy next door. Near death, he out-Duked John Wayne — and Reagan's words to the Japanese Diet: "A nuclear war cannot be won and must never be fought."

Nearby is the "Voices of Freedom"

What Mrs. Reagan wore at Washington's Gridiron Club when she wowed the press by singing "Second Hand Clothes." *(Reagan Library)*

gallery, with the names of Soviet dissidents on a metal wall above display cases. Noted Hunt: "Many of them were freed from captivity by Gorbachev from lists Reagan provided at summit meetings." You recall Reagan's words at the '91

The Oval Office as it was, 1981-89. Reagan wrote: "We were familiar with every room and hallway and had the warmest memories of our life in that beautiful, historic mansion." *(Reagan Library)*

dedication: "Today, a heroic people has cast off the chains of Marx and Lenin that gave rise to so much of this century's tensions. The iron curtain has rusted away. Totalitarianism is melting like snow. As the mythology of communism melts under the fierce heat of truth, our greatest enemy now may be complacency itself."

In his 80s, Reagan still said: "Anything I am or have done comes from Dixon." This display replicates the Gipper's boyhood living room from his beloved small-town Illinois. *(Reagan Library)*

Complacency is a library's fear. After several years, attendance drops at most presidential sites. Temporary exhibits bid to increase it. Many who saw "Madame President" or "Civil War" were first-time visitors to Simi Valley. Too, conferences like "What's Wrong with American Politics?" — and "World War II: Personal Accounts, Pearl Harbor to V-J Day," a 50th anniversary salute to U.S. involvement in World War II. It featured diaries, letters, photos, and other personal memorabilia of real people — some famous, most unknown.

Items included FDR's pince-nez, MacArthur's corncob pipe, and Hitler's last will and testament. Special events tied a vintage aircraft flyover, big band concert, and display of 1940s military vehicles. Standing, you think of U.S. military might, which Reagan restored 40 years later. "Under [him]," said Carter, "the nation stayed strong and resolute and made possible the beginning of the end of the Cold War."

LIKE FDR AND JFK, THE GIPPER grasped that people seek in rhetoric both symbolic and emotional truth. Each lights the exhibit, "Dear President Reagan," which recalls how America greeted his 1994 hand-written statement. Reagan, it learned, had Alzheimer's disease.

Tens of thousands of letters whelmed the library. All remain in its permanent archive. A visitor sees many on display, including from Spring, Texas:

"My heart ached when you gave your beautiful statement concerning your illness. I know how much courage went into that statement. I was not surprised, however, as courage you have always had! My husband [a retired U.S. Air Force pilot] was diagnosed with Alzheimer's Disease in 1987. He was 64 years old at the time ... We rode it out together, Mr. President, just as you and Nancy will do. There were many 'good days' during the next 7 years. The 'not so good days' we got through together...I wish you both God's speed throughout your journey ahead."

At the dedication, Reagan admitted to being a constant, which is not to say cockeyed, optimist — "always seeing a glass half full when some see it as half empty. And, yes, it's true — I always see the sunny side of life. And that's not just because I've been blessed by achieving so many of my dreams. My optimism comes not just from my strong faith in God, but from my strong and enduring faith in man."

You hear him, leave the library, gaze toward the Pacific, then back at the journey from Dixon to the Simi Valley, and you recall what a studio mogul said when Reagan was first suggested for governor. "No, Jimmy Stewart for governor," he said. "Ronald Reagan for best friend."

Dedication excerpts, November 4, 1991.

"For the first time, five presidents and five first ladies — past and present — have gathered together in the same locale ... As I listen to these talks I got to thinking: Wouldn't Fred Travalena, Rich Little, and Dana Carvey have a wonderful time here today?" — George Bush

"You all [the four Republican presidents] have another advantage over me. At least all of you have met another Democratic president. I've never had that opportunity yet." — Jimmy Carter

"[In 1959, Nikita] Kruschchev jabbed his finger into my chest and said: 'Your grandchildren will live under communism.' And I responded: 'Your grandchildren will live in freedom.' At that time, I was sure he was wrong. But I was not sure I was right. And now we know — thanks in great part to the strong, idealistic leadership of President Ronald Reagan, Kruschchev's grandchildren live in freedom." — Richard Nixon

"Proverbially, old men plant trees even though they do not expect to see their fruition. So it is with presidents. The doors of this library are now open and all are welcome. The judgment of history is

An historic first: Five past and present U.S. presidents in the same locale — Bush, Reagan, Carter, Ford, and Nixon at Reagan's library and museum dedication, November 4, 1991. *(Reagan Library)*

left to you—the people. I have no fears of that, for we have done our best. And so I say, come and learn from it." — Ronald Reagan

Directions: From West Los Angeles, take Interstate 405 north to the 118 Freeway west. Exit south on Madera Road and proceed to Presidential Drive. Follow signs to the Reagan Library and Museum. From Los Angeles, take U.S. Highway 101 (Ventura) north to State Highway 23 (Moorpark-Fillmore) north. From Highway 23, exit east on Olsen Road to Presidential Drive. From Pasadena, take Interstate 210 (San Fernando) to 118 Freeway west. Exit south on Madera and proceed to Presidential Drive. From Santa Barbara, take U.S. Highway 101 south to State Highway 23 north. Exit east on Olsen toward Presidential Drive.

CHAPTER 16

MR. SMOOTH
GEORGE BUSH LIBRARY
AND MUSEUM

(George Bush Library and Museum)

RETURN TO AN AMERICA OF puppies and Masonic lodges and picket fences and Sunday school — frozen in amber, but fixed and sure. It prized chary tenderness — the matronly librar-ian, uptown soda fountain, and streets of leaves, stick dams, and unlocked homes keying safety in the night. Did such an age exist? I believe so. You do not rein-vent youth at the time. Rather, George

George Bush, at the Grand Canyon. Caring deeply about the environment, the 41st president often asked America to preserve "our cathedrals of the outdoors." *(Bush Library)*

Bush loved what was then true, and real — "a nation," he later said, "closer to [TV's] 'The Waltons' than 'The Simpsons.' " Losing that, we lay griefs upon America.

Bush's mix — knowledge, sacrifice, and stoic heroism; deference, reverence, and normality — invoked what Whittaker Chambers once styled "some quality, deep-going, difficult to identify in the world's glib way, but good, and meaningful." Its Agincourt: what *Boston Globe* columnist Robert Healy called that "Yan-kee trait of competing hard, then picking your opponent up off the floor."

Bush belonged to the "Old Boy Network" of perquisite, expectation, and old-shoe chivalry. Politics esteems ego, power, and a Harold Hill type of flim-flam. Bush aired generosity — giving classmates half his lunch: his childhood name, "Have Half" — modesty, and self-deprecation.

What a conundrum wrapped in hard-to-get-a-handle-on. The moderate-old school-Northeastern-Episcopalian liked country and western music. The patrician enjoyed hunting, fishing, and horseshoes — not mythmaking, but authentic. Awkwardly, Bush warred on language. "Zippity doo-dah ... I'm on a cholesterol high ... Don't cry for me, Argentina." Yet his charm — "I'm president," he said of broccoli, "and I don't have to eat it!" — eclipsed Yale and Kennebunkport forming a mountain twang.

Bush offset privilege by seeming a regular fellow. "And that's the wonder, the wonder of this country," said Willy Loman in *The Death of a Salesman*, "that a man can end [up] with diamonds here on the basis of being liked!" What did he stand for? critics harped — aside

from grace, refusal to gloat, and reluctance to offend. As it turned out, more than the Brahmin Everests of relationship and face.

At home, Bush was alleged to lack the "vision thing." Abroad, he helped reshape the post-Cold War world. Heraclitus said a man cannot stand in the same river twice. He would have liked the man that, winking, Bush called "Mr. Smooth."

BUSH GREW UP IN GREENWICH, Connecticut, and spent each Maine summer at his family's home at Walker's Point. Six months after Pearl Harbor, he got his diploma from Phillips Academy

The president, Mrs. Bush, and dog Millie in the Oval Office. Next door was a small office where Bush worked, greeted visitors, and typed thank-yous on his portable typewriter. *(Bush Library)*

Bush — a.k.a. "Mr. Smooth" — often played 18 holes of golf in two hours. Right, he boards the presidential helicopter — Marine One — for a weekend trip to Camp David. *(Bush Library)*

at Andover. Turning 18, Bush joined the Navy, received wings and his commission, and became its youngest pilot. At 20, he was shot down and rescued by the submarine USS *Finback*. War toughened Bush. He was courageous under tension, and faced death with stark resistance. At night, he went on deck, stood watch at the bridge, and sensed "God's therapy." Bush grew up in a hurry.

After 58 combat missions, he came home, married Barbara Pierce in 1945, graduated from Yale, and packed a red Studebaker. The Connecticut Yankee went to Texas to prove himself, and started a company — Zapata Off-Shore — that pioneered oil drilling. Then, politics: Congress, two Senate losses, and a blanket of appointive posts. In 1980, Ronald Reagan chose him as vice president, and in '88 handed off to his protege. Bush beat Michael Dukakis by seven million votes.

In his inaugural, Bush vowed "to

make kinder the face of the nation and gentler the face of the world." To Bush, the bully pulpit meant example. Example meant bi-partisanship: Good will begat good will. At one point, Bush turned from the lectern and extended his hand to the Speaker of the House Jim Wright and then to Senate Majority Leader George Mitchell. "For this is the thing," he said. "This is the age of the offered hand." Later, he grasped that Democrats wanted his head, not hand.

Bush smoothed the rough edges of Reaganism. Congress passed child care, disability legislation, and a civil rights bill which — take your choice — upheld or ended quotas. The Left welcomed the first post-Carter rewrite of the Clean Air Act. The Right liked more funds for drug enforcement and Clarence Thomas on the Supreme Court. Both cheered volunteerism: of glowing memory, the "thousand points of light." Feint, jab, zig, and zag. Like FDR, Bush liked what worked.

What didn't was the Budget Pact. Bush's 1988 mantra had been, "Read my lips! ... No new taxes!" In 1990, majority Democrats told Bush to raise them or risk gridlock. Trusting Mitchell — we'll cover you politically! — he upped taxes to fuel the economy and get the issue off

Bush, with Soviet leader Mikhail Gorbachev in late 1989 off Malta. Secretary of State Baker is at right. What Bush called the Revolution of '89 literally remade the world. *(Bush Library)*

his back. "Great Nations, like great men," he had said, "must keep their word." To many, the '90 pact broke it. Too late, Bush grasped how sandbagging trapped his White House.

Bush was a businessman who understood tax rate and productivity. In strange irony, he also felt concerns of faith and spirit that stirred Grange Halls and bowling alleys. The effect might have been social and economic synergy. It wasn't: Bush favored politesse to debate. Some want polarity to stop at the water's edge. He hated it even lapping at the shore.

ABROAD, BUSH COULD FORGET the gravamen of politics. What weighed was America's role in the world. "We know what works," he said in his inaugural. "Freedom works." The premise hymned what the former United Nations ambassador, China liaison, CIA director, and globe-trotting veep called "some of the most revolutionary changes that have ever taken place."

In Britain, Margaret Thatcher resigned as prime minister. In China, Tiananmen Square invited caravans of disbelief. Hungarian playwright Imre Madach wrote *The Tragedy of Man*. The Revolution of '89 hailed his victory. Mikhail Gorbachev became president of the Soviet Union, and conceded its collapse. In November 1989, the Berlin Wall fell. Lech Walesa was voted Polish president. The ex-Evil Empire held its first multi-candidate election. Marveled Bush: "It's amazing the changes that occurred in a blink of history's eye."

At Bush's prep school graduation, Secretary of War Henry Stimson gave a speech. The U.S. soldier "should be brave without being brutal, self-confident without boasting." Bush reacted warily when the Wall collapsed. A reporter said, "Why don't you show the emotion we feel?" Unsaid: You don't insult people you hope to lead. "I wanted the Soviets' help," Bush conceded later. "I wouldn't get it by bragging." He never said "The Cold War is over" until Germany reunited — October 3, 1990.

Bush's breeding masked a poker-faced heart. On December 19, 1989, he had his writers to the residence for drinks. His grandkids were all over him. The spaniel Millie licked my hand and panted for a beer. Bush left at 7 P.M. to host a Christmas party. Rising, he said, "I feel a thousand years old." At 2 A.M., I awoke to see Press Secretary Marlin Fitzwater reveal the U.S. invasion of Panama. Meeting, we had no idea that Bush had already approved the gravest decision of his presidency. You would want him on your side playing blind-man's bluff.

Pols are said to love humanity, but hate people. By contrast, add to Bush's *sang-froid* a fine feeling for the individual. On July 11, 1989, he was scheduled to talk at Kossuth Square in Budapest. His speech staff at the White House was unaware of all-day rain. By radio the writers heard Bush begin to speak: "I have this speech in my hand, and I'm going to tear it up!" Hungarians roared as Bush ripped the speech cards — *my* cards — and raised them above his head.

Next day, we learned why he ad-libbed briefly and then waved the crowd home. Translated, the text would have lasted 40 minutes in the rain: Bush was being kind. Later, he sent me a photo that graced papers around the world: Bush, holding half the speech in one hand and the second half in the other. "It's raining in Budapest," it read. "I'll wing it." Speechwriter, or straight man? In the White House, you don't ask. You do.

BUSH WINGED LITTLE REGARD-ing America's destiny to lead. Letting the globe become a worse place would not make the U.S. a better place. On August 2, 1990, Saddam Hussein invaded Kuwait and dubbed it Iraq's 19th province. To Bush, a bully had kicked sand in

The president, tearing up the author's speech in Kossuth Square, Budapest, July 1989. Note half of the speech in each hand, the crowd's acclaim, and Bush's demoniac glee. *(Reuters)*

The Bushes, visiting U.S. troops in the Persian Gulf, November 22, 1990. Said Bush: "[This] is not a religious war … It is a Just War … in which good will prevail." *(Bush Library)*

freedom's face. He forged a U.N. Armada — "Operation Desert Shield." Iraq must withdraw "completely, immediately, and without condition"; its "aggression must not stand." On August 20, he addressed the Veterans of Foreign Wars: "Half a century ago, the world had the chance to stop a ruthless aggressor and missed it. We will not make that mistake again."

For 166 days, the president tried peacefully to remove Hussein from Kuwait. He knew what he meant to say, and said it. I often arrived at work to find Bush speeches hand- and self-written. All the ghosts now fused from Bush's past: Stimson, Andover, duty, scripture. "No one wanted war less than I," he said, "but we will see it through." Drum-banging protestors ringed the White House. Bush's own presiding bishop said force would be immoral. Some in Congress prophesied 100,000 "body bags." He shunned their hairshirt, and sought a resolution allowing him to use force. "This will not be another Viet Nam."

On January 16, 1991, "Operation Desert Shield" turned "Desert Storm." "Saddam [called] this a religious war," Bush said as the U.S. and its allies declared war, "but it is not a Christian or Jewish or Moslem war. It is a Just War …

in which good will prevail." Yellow ribbons dotted America. Headlines blurred: smart bombs and Scuds and Patriot missiles. Hussein's Mother of Battles became the Orphan of Defeats. Wrote the *Times'* Maureen Dowd: "War never leaves a ... President where it found him." Bush rocketed to the sacred from popular. "By God," he exclaimed, "we've licked the Viet Nam syndrome once and for all!"

A *USA Today* poll read, "Bush: 91 percent approval." In early March, he left for the weekend at Camp David. Staff members and families held hand-lettered signs: "The Great Liberator" and "91." It was surreal, and couldn't last. Yet such a time — America as moral sunshine! — deserved a coda, and got it months later. Bush had lost friends at Pearl Harbor. "Now, look, I have to be careful," he warned me about its 50th anniversary speech aboard thc USS *Missouri.* "I don't want to break down." Writing it, I didn't tell him that I hoped he would.

"Every 15 seconds a drop of oil still rises from the [sunken] *Arizona,*" Bush said as light danced on the Pacific. "As it spreads across the water, we recall the

Bush, addressing Congress, after the Gulf War. Said Edmund Burke of a like moment: "He may live long, he may do much, but he can never exceed what he does this day." *(Bush Library)*

ancient poet: 'In our sleep, pain that cannot forget falls drop by drop upon the heart.' It is as though God Himself were crying."

Bush's church was self-effacement, not spectacle. Yet his peroration linked Battleship Row and its gun turret, still visible, and the flag, flying proudly from a blessed shrine.

"Look into your hearts, and minds. You will see boys who this day became men, and men who became heroes. Look into the water here. One day — in what now seems another lifetime — it wrapped its arms around the finest sons any Nation could ever have, and carried them to another world.

"God bless them," he said, his voice cracking a third time. "God bless America — the most wondrous land on earth."

Fearing emotion, Bush bared it on December 7, 1991 — and showed himself the kind of president America should have, and needs. The memory jarred during the free fall ahead.

IN BUSH'S STUDY HUNG A PAINTing. "The Peacemakers" showed Lincoln and his generals near the end of the Civil War. Outside, battle rages. A rainbow denotes the passing of the storm.

Bush was a peacemaker. The storm was a re-election which confused and then unhorsed him. History will ask how the Bush of Desert Storm got 37.5 percent of the vote in November 1992. The why is that Bush was a world statesman and tepid politician. He hated campaigning's carousel — self-disclose, grandstand, fake intimacy — where "authenticity," said the writer Horace Busby, "is less regarded than embezzlement or murder." Politics is bloodletting. In 1992, much of it was Bush's own.

Image has spooky powers. America and aides glimpsed a different man. Bush was unhip, which remains endearing: Pac-Man was a camper, not video game. He asked Aretha Franklin's phonetic spelling, and called "R-E-S-P-E-C-T" "respect." To Little Leaguers, Bush read — his idea — from *The Encyclopedia of Baseball*. "Wanna' know about Yaz [Carl Yastrzemski]? 'Ya gotta have this book." Was America's oldest teenager 68, or 18? Hearing Bush, Andy Hardy lilted through the mind. He liked kids, comity — the Leader of the Free World rose at 5 A.M. to type thank-you notes — honest sentiment, and family. Barbara Bush spoke daily with their five children across the country.

Millions would have cheered had they known. Why didn't they? Reticence: Bush's core lay in the heart, not sleeve. The economy dove in 1990-91, then turned. Bush got the blame, not credit. Confusion hurt selling — "Message: I care." Bill Clinton called himself a "new Democrat." The press panted to agree.

The private and public man. At left, the Bushes and spaniel Millie, at Kennebunkport. Bush often joked about his identity crisis as "Barbara's husband or Millie's co-owner." Both wrote best-selling books. Below, a tear-streaked day. The president at Pearl Harbor, aboard the USS *Missouri*, December 7, 1991. *(Bush Library)*

★ ★ WINDOWS ON THE WHITE HOUSE ★ ★

In 1979, Erma Bombeck wrote, "It hasn't happened yet, but it's inevitable. One night, [an actress] will lean over the footlights of a Broadway theatre and in the childlike voice of Peter Pan ask, 'Will everyone who believes in Tinker Bell clap your hands?' And the theatre will resound in silence. The silence will record the [end of] faith in America." In 1991, America clapped for George Bush. In 1992, it lost faith.

FOR A WHILE, BUSH BROODED about his loss. "I couldn't get through. I'd say, 'Good news, the economy is recovering,' and there would be all these people saying, 'Bush is out of touch.' I couldn't jump over the hurdle." In time, he cleared it to refind family, friends, and freedom.

"Just think," he said, shining cowboy boots, "I don't need new suits for the rest of my life." He got new support in a 1994 Gallup Poll. Fifty-eight percent approved of Bush's handling of his job — after JFK, post-1960's highest-rated president. In turn, Bush approved of liberation/retirement. No more handlers! Ignore the spin doctors! Forget photo opportunities!

Mrs. Bush wrote a best-selling book. Her husband retook to golf: "Now that I'm no longer president, it's amazing how many people beat me." He passed a new rule: Nearing grandpa, his 14 grandchildren must "deimperialize the presidential retirement" by giving him a hug. The family divided time between Houston and Kennebunkport. Each evoked the most overwhelming sense of coming home to some locale that belonged.

In 1993, Bush was Knighted by Her Majesty Queen Elizabeth. Back in Houston, he asked Barbara, "How does it feel to be married to a real Knight?" His wife said, "Sir George, make the coffee." Today, it is not hard to make people realize what kind of man, and president, that George Bush was.

George Bush Library and Museum. David Alsobrook, Director. Texas A&M University. College Station, Texas 77843-1145. Phone: (409) 260-9552. Fax: (409) 260-9557. Web site: http://csdl.tamu.edu/bushlib/.

Hours: Monday through Saturday, 9:30 A.M. to 5:30 P.M. Sunday, noon to 5 P.M. Open every day, except New Year's Day, Thanksgiving, and Christmas. Admission: Children age 16 years and under, free. Age 17 years and older, $3. Seniors age 62 and over, $2. A & M students with identification, $2.50. A & M and Blinn College faculty, $2.50. Groups, $2.50. Free parking. Library gift shop is open during regular hours.

★ ★ MR. SMOOTH ★ ★

Overhead model of the Bush Library and Museum, dedicated on November 6, 1997, on 90 acres of Texas A&M University. It is the 12th presidential library to open to the public. *(Texas A&M University)*

"THIS LIBRARY WILL DESCRIBE global and national events in nearly 45,000 feet of archival and office space and almost 25,000 feet of public exhibition space," George Bush said of his center which opened in 1997, at Texas A&M University, in College Station. "It will feature the latest in computer wizardry. I'm still trying, without much luck, to learn Nintendo from my ten-year-old grandson Sam."

The newest Mr. Wizard presidential library links a museum, archives, Centers for Presidential, Leadership, and International Studies, and classroom space for the Departments of Economics, Sociology, and Political Science. Add to the above a Gulf War exhibit, replica of Bush's Air Force One and Camp David offices, and residence for the Bushes when they visit College Station.

"I plan to use this library for my own research," said America's newest former president. "I plan to do some writing

Part of the A&M campus at College Station, Texas. Said then-Governor-elect George W. Bush at the library's 1994 groundbreaking: "This is absolutely the right site." *(Texas A&M University)*

there and I would like to do some teaching, because when you teach, you learn." Rim-shot, and *déjà vu.* "How's that for a 'vision thing'?"

Several presidential libraries are tied to major universities. The man who called himself the "Education President" had four sites vie for his. Yale, Bush's alma mater. Rice, in Houston, his adopted city. The University of Houston. A&M won because of what it was — like Bush, Texan, military, and ramrod-straight — and what it bid.

Bush, speaking to the Texas A&M cadets shortly before leaving the presidency in January 1993. *(Texas A&M University)*

Texas A&M ranks among the top 10 schools in National Science Foundation research and number of national merit finalists. Bush liked its university corps of cadets, football's "Twelfth Man," and "Gig 'em Aggie" yell to more than 40,000 students and 200,000 active alumni. Magnetic, too: A&M's history — a land-grant university — and the center's 90-acre beauty — hard by a creek, among a grove of oak trees, on the school's 5,200-acre campus.

Most of all — call it decency, patrimony, or simple scholarship — Bush liked A&M's proposal to link politics and public service. It enhanced the library with an academic curricula: the George Bush School of Government and Public Service. College Station now offers a master's of public administration degree.

"I hope my life has demonstrated a commitment to public service that was inculcated into me very early on by my father, and into him by his father," Bush has said. "We believe in this concept of public service. So in this new school ... this new academic enterprise ... we can highlight what motivated people to be in public service ... I am personally very interested in that."

So was Texas A&M, pledging $40 million — nearly half the center's cost.

THE KENNEDY SCHOOL OF GOVernment hails the Camelot that was and/

or is. Like Texas — the state, not university — Bush's offers students a sprawling map of courses. Among them are Literacy, Government Ethics, Political Competition, Economic Competition, Development of the Southwest Region, Energy Development and Policy, China and the Far East, and the United Nations.

The center will feature conferences and symposia, and an institute to study government transition. Bush, himself transferred on January 20, 1993, hopes that, "The years of our Administration

will be treated kindly, but fairly. I know this: Our library will be fair in expressing the change that happened as the world turned upside down."

Not all libraries — e.g. Nixon's — serve as archives for presidential papers. Bush's does. Like the rest, it houses correspondence with other presidents. Texas A&M will also create and fund an Oral and Visual History program etching the creed and career of the 41st president.

"James Joyce once wrote that, 'The past is consumed in the present and the

The George Bush Library and Museum foyer. Said Bush: "The [library] will examine up-close American leadership during a period of unprecedented global transformation." *(Texas A&M University)*

present is alive only because it gives birth to the future,'" said former Canadian Prime Minister Brian Mulroney. "Nothing better illustrates ... the majestic cycle of human life and personal endeavor, than [our] tribute to the public service of George Bush" — son of a U.S. senator, Navy flyer, congressman, director, ambassador, veep, and president.

Presidential libraries are a unique institution. "Americans," Bush observed, "have built [them] to record what they've done, and express what they are. These institutions mirror the Nation they span." The center writes the nation's post-war life, demise of Communism, and birth of a new world order — "documentation for some of the most revolutionary changes that man has ever seen.

"Whether it is the [Mideast] peace talks ... or whether it is the unification of Germany ... whether it is the decline or fall of the Soviet Empire ... whether it is the historic precedence-setting coalition for Desert Storm. All of that will be reflected with accurate detail in the library for scholars to make their own conclusion."

Like all libraries, Bush's hopes that scholars — also, public officials, visiting lecturers, distinguished and post-doctoral fellows, and A&M faculty and students — will reach *its* conclusion. "The library," said Don Wilson, executive director of the Bush Library Center, "em-

bodies Bush's respect for the family, fidelity to education, belief in the global economy, and idea that government service is an honorable calling where officials must show honor and respect."

Next door, the museum will serve Bush through exhibits, family bric-a-brac, kids activities, and display of family books, videos, and computer goingson. "It's interesting," said Bush, "how individuals learn different things at different stages. For instance, Barbara taught me, as the Good Book says, 'to act justly, and walk humbly.' Believe me, I am in the wake of her best-seller" — 1994's *A Memoir*. Already, the thing that College Station has learned is to wed policy and legacy.

The conference center will host issues from energy and education to clean air, national security, the disabled, and privatization. "People will come here to study and debate," Bush said, "as they have for years in other presidential libraries — all older than me, though I'm starting to wonder."

Recently, he observed, "I was in a Houston barbershop. Two little kids were staring at me as they peeked around a corner. One said, 'No, it is not.' The other said, 'Yes, it is. I'm sure that's him. You can tell by the wrinkles.'"

Self-effacement, not aggrandizement, from a politician? Perhaps Bush tells about himself by simply recounting the tale.

★ ★ WINDOWS ON THE WHITE HOUSE ★ ★

WRINKLES ARE LARGELY ACA-demic in two programs of the Bush School of Government and Public Service. The Center for Presidential Studies will supplement library holdings with data bases not available in traditional archives. The Center for Leadership Studies will fix leadership, its traits and criteria, and links between leaders and followers in a modern democracy.

"The history that we made in this administration," Bush said, "I'd like students to learn." History, Richard Nixon told Henry Kissinger, depends on who writes it. The library's depends on who sees it. It will show the Bushes in their Studebaker off for Texas in '48 — Chancellor Helmut Kohl saying that German reunification could not have happened without Bush — Bush on rhetoric: "The Bible mentions the Burning Bush, but I'm not that hot a speaker" — and recalling how the Iron Lady helped repel Saddam Hussein.

"Margaret Thatcher was at Aspen in August 1990 when Iraq invaded Kuwait," Bush will tell you. "She was one of the first persons I turned to, and she never let me down. One day I called to explain why I had decided not to interdict a merchant ship off Oman. She listened to my explanation, agreed with the decision, then added these words of caution that guided me through the Gulf: 'Remember, George, this is no time to go wobbly.'"

You will not see Bush wobbly in America's newest presidential library. Instead, hail Millie's co-owner/next-door neighbor/reshaper of the world/hero of Desert Storm/model dad/grandpa extraordinaire/husband of America's *Grandmere*/parachute jumper — at 72, in 1997 — to relive his World War II leap of a half-century earlier.

"The definition of a successful life," he often said, "must include serving others." Think of the center as $82 million of hug a child, touch a life, stir a heart, and help thy neighbor. You might not be prudent to call this Bush's greatest Point of Light. But you might be right.

Groundbreaking excerpts, November 30, 1994.

"Think about the kaleidoscope of social and political change during our four years: The fall of the Berlin Wall, and the reunification of Germany; the dismantling of the Soviet State; the historic coalition that ejected Saddam Hussein from Kuwait; the good-faith dialogue of a lasting peace between age-old enemies in the Middle East. We faced a new world every day, it seemed, and the archives will help show how we answered the call to lead as no other nation could." — George Bush

The author, with President and Mrs. Bush at Christmas 1990. Below, meeting in the White House residence December 19, 1989 — the night that American troops invaded Panama. *(Bush Library)*

"As Prime Minister of Canada for nine years, I worked as closely with George Bush as Vice President and President as any other leader in the world — perhaps even more so. I saw him, privately, up-close, when great decisions of peace and war were made. I saw him at crucial G7 summits around the world, at NATO meetings in time of crisis — and around the swimming pool at Kennebunkport when our major problem was explaining to the media why the fish had avoided us for another day!" — Brian Mulroney

"In our family, the torch has been passed to our sons — the Governor-elect of Texas and a rising star in Florida. My political days are behind me. Life for Barbara and me now means spending more time enjoying our family, and trying to be Points of Light in our community. But we want to do more, and I look forward to coming to this school ... I want to share with students my thoughts on public service — that service to country is a noble calling; that there is much more to it than elections and sound bites; that it means helping others and sacrificing and contributing to a cause larger than yourself." — George Bush

"When President Bush was beginning to focus on the magnitude and complexity of this [Gulf War] crisis in the immediate wake of the invasion, he invited me to the White House for a private evening of

highly confidential discussions ... He set out for me his views on keeping NATO solidarity intact; defined the potential umbrella role that the United Nations Security Council had to play; discussed how our personal relations with moderate Arab leaders could be used to ensure their indispensable participation in repelling Saddam Hussein; and forecast a battle wherein we would prevail — and here I am quoting him directly — 'if we strike swiftly and overwhelmingly from the air.' That conversation took place a full six months before the War began." — Brian Mulroney

Directions: From Houston, take Highway 290 north to Hempstead. Go north on Highway 6 to Bryan. At College Station, take Business 6 (Texas Avenue) to second light and turn left on FM2818. Go to George Bush Drive. Turn right and proceed to the Bush Library and Museum. From Dallas, take Interstate 45 south. Exit at Madisonville/Highway 21, turn right on 21, and go south through Madisonville. Take FM2818 south to George Bush Drive. Turn left and follow signs. From Austin, take Highway 290 east. Exit at Highway 21 and go to Caldwell/Bryan. Turn right on 2818 in Bryan and proceed to George Bush Drive. Turn left and proceed to the library and museum.

CHAPTER 17

IF

PLATO SAID, "BEFORE WE TALK, let us first define our terms." Choose the most literate, or volcanic, of the 12 library presidents. Who made the muses dance? By contrast, who rivaled Sominex? Who made of the office existential pleasure, and for whom, and why?

Each president can be judged pathetic or a paladin. Knowing truth, God leaves to us opinion. So suspend history, embrace fantasy, and indulge a howclose, oh-but, what-might-have-been frame of mind.

What person might have, but did not, become president — depriving America of his or her skill and this book of his library? A British prime minister observed, "Your representative owes you, not only his industry alone, but his judgment."

Sit back, pull up a chair, and judge how presidents judge.

"The elections of delegates to the Chicago Republican convention show [James G.] Blaine to be the favorite candidate. He fails in two points ... He lacks

James G. Blaine

the confidence of thoughtful, high-minded, and patriotic people. They doubt his personal integrity; they think he is a demagogue ... Either [Senator George F.] Edmunds, [Secretary of War Robert Todd] Lincoln, or [Senator John] Sherman would be a better president and a better candidate. He does not belong to the class of leaders of whom Hamilton, Jefferson, Clay, Calhoun, Seward, Lincoln, and Webster are types ... Clay would rather be right than be president. Blaine would gladly be wrong to be president. I still hope Edmunds may be the nominee, or Lincoln, or Sherman." (Blaine was

nominated, but lost to Grover Cleveland.)
— Rutherford B. Hayes, 1884

Charles Evans Hughes

"[Supreme Court Justice] Charles Evans Hughes would have been a great president. He nearly made it [in 1916, losing California late on Election Night and, thus, the presidency to Woodrow Wilson]. He would have brought probity and intelligence to the Oval Office. What a a rare combination in his, or any, age." — Herbert Hoover, 1955

"We see many things alike. I admire him [Wendell Willkie]. I think he understands that we ought to have two parties — one liberal and the other conservative. As it is now, each party is split by dissenters … Let the conservatives have their own voice. From the liberals of both parties Willkie and I together can form a new, really liberal party in America."— Franklin Roosevelt, 1944

Richard Russell

"Senator [Richard] Russell is without any question an able and an intelligent man. He has been governor of Georgia and is now senator from that great state. He has all the qualifications as to ability and brains. But he is poison to northern Democrats and honest liberals. I doubt if he could carry a single state north of the Ohio River … Too bad he had to be born in Georgia, home of the modern Ku Klux Klan and the most vicious of anti-Catholics. He would have been a great president."— Harry S. Truman, 1952

"When a committee from the Board of Trustees of Columbia University asked me to consider becoming president of that great institution, I said — as I did later when other people had ideas about another presidency — that they were talking to the wrong Eisenhower. My brother Milton was uniquely fitted for leadership because of his scholarly depth and his lifelong work in principal areas of American life — governmental, economic, and academic."— Dwight D. Eisenhower, 1963

Robert F. Kennedy, Jr.

"First, he [Robert F. Kennedy, Jr.] has high moral standards, strict personal ethics. He's a puritan, absolutely incorruptible. Then he has this terrific executive energy. We've got more guys around here with ideas. The problem is to get things done. Bobby's the best organizer I've ever seen. He's got compassion, a real sense of compassion. Those Cuban prisoners [after the Bay of Pigs] ... weighed on his mind for 18 months. His loyalty comes next ... I've always wanted to get the best men, and they don't come any better than Bobby."— John F. Kennedy, 1963

"[Long-time Speaker of the House Sam Rayburn] taught me that narrow majorities in a legislative body can, with leadership, produce results that far outstrip their numbers. 'With a big, unwieldy majority on your side,' Mr. Rayburn used to say, 'half your people are back home campaigning, or off on vacation someplace because they don't think their individual votes are that important. But with a thin majority, you can develop a strong sense of party discipline and be assured that every man will be on the floor for a crucial vote.' Government is legislation, and no one grasped that like Mr. Sam. He was like a daddy to me."— Lyndon B. Johnson, 1971

Thomas Dewey

"I would rate Tom Dewey [1943-55 governor of New York] in that category [those who should have become president]. I campaigned for him in 1948 when I was a congressman. I got to know him very well later throughout my period as vice president and my years out of office. And also till he died [1971] when I was president.

"He had some extraordinarily good qualities. Above everything else, in addition to his own high intelligence, he picked very good people. The Dewey people on his staff were outstanding. He was confident enough of his own ability that he wasn't afraid to pick people that were as smart as he was. And that's the mark of an executive.

"Dewey was a first-class geopolitical thinker. He understood foreign policy, and his judgment was excellent. Finally, I liked Dewey because he was about in the same mainstream of politics that I was. I mean, I wasn't against [conservative Senator Robert] Taft — but Dewey had the same views, for example, on civil rights that I did. A more, shall we say, progressive view than some of the Republicans. Dewey would have made a great president, no question."
— Richard Nixon, 1991

"It's very hard to pick one person out of the many people that I knew for my 30 years in political life. I would say from a technical point of view, Tom Dewey — if he'd been elected in 1948 — would have been a superb president. He knew government. He knew our Constitution. He had great experience in working with the legislative body. He would have, in my judgment, fallen into the Washington environment — despite its difficulties — and done a good job.

Everett Dirksen

"On the other hand, if you had wanted someone who grew up in the Washington political arena, who knew Congress, understood the Congressional and White House relationship — Everett Dirksen, the Senator from Illinois, would have been terrific. And one final individual. I'm prejudiced: He came from Michigan. Arthur Vandenberg was outstanding in the field of foreign policy, and as a leader in the Senate. He would have had a great background to be president.

Arthur Vandenberg

"So those three who never got to be president might well have done a good job as president." — Gerald Ford, 1995

Walter Mondale

"I'll never forget what [close friend and lawyer] Charles Kirbo told me down in Plains that [1976] month when I was interviewing vice-presidential candidates. He said that some presidents, like Johnson, were always worried about the vice president overshadowing them, but he said that no one could overshadow a president and that what I should do is pick someone whom I could get along with, who could help me with my problems, and be president someday if anything happened to me. He was right, and Fritz [Walter Mondale] has been extremely helpful and terribly loyal, even when he disagreed."— Jimmy Carter, 1981

"When I was asked to be the co-chairman of Barry Goldwater's 1964 presidential campaign in California, I didn't hesitate a moment. I'd met Barry at the home of [wife] Nancy's parents in Phoenix several years before and admired him greatly. His book, *The Conscience of a Conservative*, contained a lot of the same points I'd been making in my speeches and I strongly believed the country needed him. As I said in a speech that year, 'He has faith that you and I have the ability and the dignity and the right to make our own decisions and determine our own destiny.'" — Ronald Reagan, 1990

Barry Goldwater

"I would have to go with Tom Dewey in 1948. He was a stiff and formal candidate, but his record as governor and as a prosecutor was superb. In my view, Dewey would have been strong in foreign affairs, and would have worked for better domestic answers than the Fair Deal type embraced by Truman and company. We'll never know, but Dewey is my choice." — George Bush, 1996

CHAPTER 18

FINALE

THE BOXER JOE LOUIS ONCE said of an opponent, "He can run, but he can't hide." Presidents can't, either. The office was their ring. At libraries, visitors act as referee. Does the library reflect the man I knew? — for we think we know our presidents. Does it inflate him, or present his scars? Do I leave thinking more of him, or less — and to what avail, and why?

"He won honorable distinction," biographer Charles R. Williams wrote of Rutherford B. Hayes, "[and] the popularity which runs after, not that which is fought for." Libraries seek popularity — and to catch their subject at high tide.

No harm. You don't expect them to welcome blame. Take what they give, add memory and (re)appraisal, and their legacy may become more clear.

A college professor said, "Perspective is all." I hope that *Windows on the White House* will enhance perspective. My purpose has been less to praise than illumine these presidential libraries — for they are a part of us, and we of them.

For good or ill, each strives to convince, sail freedom's ship, and make history move its way. "One generation plants the seed," says a Chinese proverb. "Another gets the shade." Come, learn, and treasure America's inchoate past.

POSTLOGUE

This appendix lists the presidential libraries, the birth and burial sites of their subjects, and foundations and other nonprofit organizations devoted to their study. All welcome newcomers, and their contributions and membership fees are non-deductible.

LIBRARIES

Rutherford B. Hayes Center
Presidency: 1877-81
Dedication date: May 30, 1916
Location: Fremont, Ohio
Annual visitors: 38,794
Area: 45,200 square feet

Herbert Hoover Library-Museum
Presidency: 1929-33
Dedication date: August 10, 1962
Location: West Branch, Iowa
Annual visitors: 84,964
Area: 44,500 square feet

Franklin D. Roosevelt Library
Presidency: 1933-45
Dedication date: June 30, 1941
Location: Hyde Park, New York
Annual visitors: 153,345
Area: 40,539 square feet

Harry S. Truman Library
Presidency: 1945-53

Dedication date: July 6, 1957
Location: Independence, Missouri
Annual visitors: 152,430
Area: 60,865 square feet

Dwight D. Eisenhower Library
Presidency: 1953-61
Dedication date: May 1, 1962
Location: Abilene, Kansas
Annual visitors: 82,190
Area: 81,466 square feet

John Fitzgerald Kennedy Library
Presidency: 1961-63
Dedication date: October 20, 1979
Location: Boston, Massachusetts
Annual visitors: 190, 296
Area: 71,847 square feet

Lyndon Baines Johnson Library and Museum
Presidency: 1963-1969
Dedication date: May 22, 1971
Location: University of Texas,

Austin, Texas
Annual visitors: 368,175
Area: 96,981 square feet.

Richard Nixon Library and Birthplace
Presidency: 1969-74
Dedication date: July 19, 1990
Location: Yorba Linda, California
Annual visitors: 240,000
Area: 52,000 square feet

Gerald R. Ford Library
Presidency: 1974-77
Dedication date: April 27, 1981
Location: University of Michigan,
Ann Arbor, Michigan
Annual researchers: 800
Area: 35,532 square feet

Gerald R. Ford Museum
Dedication date: September 18, 1981
Location: Grand Rapids, Michigan
Annual visitors: 91,934
Area: 35,259 square feet

Jimmy Carter Library
Presidency: 1977-1981
Dedication date: October 1, 1986
Location: Atlanta, Georgia
Annual visitors: 68,315
 Area: 63,475 square feet

Ronald Reagan Library and Museum
Presidency: 1981-89
Dedication date: November 4, 1991
Location: Simi Valley, California
Annual visitors: 140,518

Area: 91,193 square feet

George Bush Library and Museum
Presidency: 1989-93
Dedication date: November 6, 1997
Location: Texas A&M University,
College Station, Texas
Area: 70,000 square feet

BIRTH/BURIAL SITES
Rutherford B. Hayes (1822-1893)
Born: Delaware, Ohio
Historical marker
Buried: Rutherford B. Hayes
Presidential Center in Fremont, Ohio

Herbert Hoover (1874-1964)
Born: West Branch, Iowa
Open to the public
Buried: Herbert Hoover Library-
Museum in West Branch

Franklin D. Roosevelt (1882-1945)
Born: Hyde Park, New York
Open to the public
Buried: Franklin D. Roosevelt Library
in Hyde Park

Harry S. Truman (1884-1972)
Born: Lamar, Missouri
Open to the public
Buried: Harry S. Truman Library in
Independence, Missouri

Dwight D. Eisenhower (1890-1969)
Born: Denison, Texas

★ ★ POSTLOGUE ★ ★

Open to the public
Buried: Dwight D. Eisenhower
Library in Abilene, Kansas

John F. Kennedy (1917-1963)
Born: Brookline, Massachusetts
Open to the public
Buried: Arlington National Cemetery
in Arlington, Virginia

Lyndon B. Johnson (1908-1973)
Born: Stonewall, Texas
Open to the public
Buried: Lyndon B. Johnson National
Historical Park in Stonewall

Richard M. Nixon (1913-1994)
Born: Yorba Linda, California
Open to the public
Buried: Richard Nixon Library and
Birthplace, Yorba Linda

Gerald R. Ford (1913-)
Born: Omaha, Nebraska
Historical marker

Jimmy Carter (1924-)
Born: Plains, Georgia
Hospital closed to tourists

Ronald Reagan (1911-)
Born: Tampico, Illinois
Open to the public

George Bush (1924-)
Born: Milton, Massachusetts
Historical marker

FOUNDATIONS

Ohio Historical Society
(Harding Home, Hayes Center)
1982 Velma Avenue
Columbus, Ohio 43211
(800) 686-1541

Western Reserve Historical Society
(Lawnfield)
10825 East Boulevard
Cleveland, Ohio 44106
(216) 721-5722

*Herbert Hoover Presidential
Library Association*
Box 696
West Branch, Iowa 52358-0696
(319) 643-5327

*Franklin and Eleanor Roosevelt
Institute*
511 Albany Post Road
Hyde Park, New York 12538
(914) 229-8114

Harry S. Truman Institute
U.S. Highway 24 and Delaware
Independence, Missouri 64050
(816) 833-1400

Eisenhower Foundation
The Eisenhower Center
Abilene, Kansas 67410
(913) 263-4751

*The John F. Kennedy
Library Foundation*
Columbia Point

Boston, Massachusetts 02125
(617) 929-4523

LBJ Foundation
LBJ Library and Museum
2313 Red River Street
Austin, Texas 78705
(512) 482-5279

The Nixon Library Associates' Club
The Nixon Library
18001 Yorba Linda Boulevard
Yorba Linda, California 92686
(714) 993-5075

The Gerald Ford Foundation
Gerald R. Ford Library
1000 Beal Avenue
Ann Arbor, Michigan 48109
(313) 741-2218

Carter Presidential Center
One Copenhill Avenue
Atlanta, Georgia 30307
(404) 331-3900

The Ronald Reagan Foundation
The Reagan Presidential Library
40 Presidential Drive
Simi Valley, California 93065
(805) 522-8511

*Ronald Reagan Home Preservation
Foundation*
Box 816
Dixon, Illinois 61021
(815) 288-3404

*George Bush Presidential Library
Foundation*
c/o Texas A&M University
Mail Stop 1145
College Station, Texas 77843-1145
(409) 862-2251

For more information, contact: Office of Presidential Libraries, Assistant Archivist for Presidential Libraries, National Archives and Records Administration, Washington, D.C. 20408. Phone: (202) 501-5700. Fax: (202) 501-5709.

BIBLIOGRAPHY

Alsop, Joseph, *FDR: A Centenary Remembrance*. New York: The Viking Press, 1982.

Ambrose, Stephen E., *Eisenhower: Soldier and President*. New York: Simon and Schuster, 1990.

__, *Nixon* (Three volumes). New York: Simon and Schuster, 1987.

Cannon, Lou, *President Reagan: The Role of a Lifetime*. New York: Simon and Schuster, 1991.

Carter, Jimmy, *Why Not the Best?* Nashville: Broadman Press, 1975.

Daniels, Jonathan, *The Man of Independence*. Philadelphia: J.B. Lipincott Company, 1950.

Ford, Gerald R., *A Time to Heal*. New York: Harper & Row, 1979.

Green, Fitzhugh, *George Bush: An Intimate Portrait*. New York: Hippocrene Books, 1989.

Hoogenboom, Ari, *The Presidency of Rutherford B. Hayes*. Lawrence: University Press of Kansas, 1988.

Hoover, Herbert, *The Memoirs of Herbert Hoover* (Three Volumes). New York: The Macmillan Company, 1951-52.

Johnson, Lyndon B., *The Vantage Point*. New York: Holt, Rinehart, and Winston, 1971.

King, Nicolas, *George Bush: A Biography*. New York: Dodd, Mead, 1980.

Lash, Joseph P., *Eleanor and Franklin*. New York: W.W. Norton and Co., 1971.

Leuchtenburg, William E., *The LIFE History of the United States*. New York: TIME-LIFE Books, 1976.

Manchester, William, *One Brief Shining Moment*. Boston: Little, Brown and Company, 1983.

McCullough, David, *Truman*. New York: Simon and Schuster, 1992.

Morgan, Ted, *FDR: A Biography*. New York: Simon and Schuster, 1986.

Morris, Willie, *North Toward Home*. Boston: Houghton Mifflin, 1967.

Nixon, Richard, *Richard Nixon in the Arena: A Memoir of Victory, Defeat, and Renewal*. New York: Simon and Schuster, 1990.

__, *The Memoirs of Richard Nixon*. New York: Grosset and Dunlap, 1978.

Reagan, Ronald, *An American Life*. New York: Simon and Schuster, 1990.

Schlesinger, Arthur M. Jr., *A Thousand Days: John F. Kennedy in the White House*. Cambridge: Houghton Mifflin, 1965.

Smith, Richard Norton, *Thomas E. Dewey and His Times*. New York: Simon and Schuster, 1982.

Smithsonian Exposition Books, *Every Four Years*. New York: W.W. Norton and Company, 1980.

Truman, Harry S., *Memoirs*. Garden City: Doubleday, 1955-56.

White, Theodore H., *In Search of History*. New York: Harper and Row, 1978.

__, *The Making of the President 1960*. New York: Atheneum, 1961.

Williams, Harry T., *Hayes of the Twenty-Third: The Civil War Officer*. New York: Alfred A. Knopf, 1965.

MUSEUM VISITORS

OFFICE OF PRESIDENTIAL LIBRARIES

Year	Hayes	Hoover	Roosevelt	Truman	Eisenhower	Kennedy	Johnson	Nixon	Ford	Carter	Reagan	TOTAL
1970	27,000	91,083	162,423	182,823	449,631							912,960
1971	25,000	70,648	160,295	186,174	263,234		85,240					790,591
1972	31,000	81,989	181,520	187,866	318,684		676,116					1,477,175
1973	29,000	82,822	191,194	340,818	299,741		704,190					1,647,765
1974	30,000	84,002	194,314	264,230	215,586		542,717					1,330,849
1975	25,000	106,109	188,106	291,180	197,727		520,985					1,329,107
1976	26,000	148,099	223,673	510,584	295,532		905,244					2,109,132
1977	23,000	91,324	371,514	321,136	177,332		657,907					1,642,213
1978	25,000	95,418	276,865	264,714	170,172		502,115					1,334,284
1979	22,167	69,775	215,582	219,067	127,026		480,521					1,134,038
1980	23,361	64,088	241,459	201,642	143,910	563,470	446,062					1,683,994
1981	25,809	70,337	226,238	211,864	125,458	357,724	384,884		22,476			1,424,790
1982	29,909	61,227	202,048	197,477	131,961	291,430	368,289		423,886			1,706,227
1983	33,912	59,637	206,147	200,913	117,420	222,847	409,304		183,071			1,433,251
1984	37,738	58,487	186,833	210,149	109,720	243,173	357,390		139,529			1,343,019
1985	34,690	50,310	194,578	188,552	115,103	215,790	402,768		114,214			1,316,005
1986	35,698	51,958	193,150	176,578	101,232	190,586	447,714		92,526			1,289,442
1987	36,356	53,690	189,335	168,645	95,895	212,582	419,595		97,812	190,388		1,464,298
1988	34,132	95,653	167,747	159,119	90,201	206,115	318,422		95,785	117,881		1,285,055
1989	33,771	104,483	184,964	155,182	96,180	210,318	420,199		81,385	86,440		1,372,921
1990	39,885	99,741	168,898	149,521	158,058	199,927	342,951	200,000	83,353	79,668		1,522,002
1991	42,206	71,833	163,237	136,864	125,345	175,076	308,033	200,000	120,460	85,749		1,428,803
1992	46,643	75,704	168,514	139,230	93,287	213,996	388,529	200,000	88,419	86,383	280,219	1,780,924
1993	45,829	84,964	153,345	152,430	82,190	189,566	368,175	200,000	91,934	68,315	140,518	1,577,266
1994	38,794	89,998	136,268	139,399	98,000	261,783	256,670	400,000	89,216	68,975	152,887	1,701,990
1995	44,212	83,700	171,307	119,028	86,546	271,608	260,219	200,000	89,815	78,898	182,085	1,587,418
1996	45,711	78,201	159,347	132,402	192,000	300,000	274,190	200,000	90,000	77,865	150,000	1,699,716
TOTAL	891,723	2,175,274	4,828,901	5,607,587	4,477,171	4,325,991	11,248,429	1,400,000	1,903,881	940,562	905,709	39,325,235
To date	1,714,735	2,689,821	9,189,054	7,417,708	6,354,694	4,325,991	11,248,429	1,400,000	1,903,881	940,562	905,709	48,090,584

APPENDIX

PRINCIPAL HOLDINGS OF THE PRESIDENTIAL LIBRARIES

	Hayes Library	Hoover Library	Roosevelt Library	Truman Library	Eisenhower Library	Kennedy Library	Johnson Library	Nixon Project	Ford Library	Carter Library	Reagan Library	TOTAL
MANUSCRIPTS (pgs.)												
Personal Papers	3,800,000	7,125,715	16,323,943	14,050,024	21,099,660	29,813,996	32,643,672	784,000	18,890,168	27,319,430	4,108,500	175,959,108
Federal Records	0	153,303	710,000	713,600	693,300	645,967	2,848,756	912,000	719,000	324,000	280,000	7,999,926
Presidential Records	0	0	0	0	0	0	0	44,414,000	0	0	42,419,650	86,833,650
AUDIOVISUAL												
Still Pictures (images)	75,000	42,071	134,259	92,287	211,277	144,042	617,878	435,000	318,336	1,500,253	1,604,070	5,174,473
Film (feet)	1,040	155,591	308,676	331,499	617,825	7,162,122	824,777	2,200,000	785,106	1,120,080	542,750	14,049,466
Video Tape (hours)	55	137	28	125	179	1,249	8,044	3,900	1,474	1,434	18,482	35,107
Audio Tape (hours)	120	502	1,024	285	1,073	7,310	13,247	1,490	1,527	2,000	13,200	41,778
Audio Discs (hours)	600	78	1,108	436	277	725	808	0	52	0	815	4,899
ORAL HISTORY												
Pages	75	11,864	3,120	53,015	31,432	55,079	58,424	2,200	954	3,606	78	219,847
Hours	10	0	84	1,470	787	2,353	2,483	228	32	548	0	7,995
MUSEUM OBJECTS	13,958	5,477	23,691	25,704	32,173	16,654	37,105	21,750	8,184	40,000	75,075	299,771
PRINTED MATERIALS												
Books (volumes)	73,000	21,141	44,346	38,212	24,042	74,248	16,673	9,022	9,475	2,592	15,438	328,189
Serials (volumes/titles)	2,714	23,887	25,370	67,219	25,082	12,354	4,708	0	321	3,375	38,945	203,975
Microform (rolls/cards)	13,751	1,489	2,493	1,476	5,169	4,638	4,411	0	7,355	6,791	4,577	52,150
Other (items)	5,250	1,451	82,669	96,110	24,456	13,139	25,738	0	2,648	7,420	13,500	272,381

INDEX

Numbers in italics refer to illustrations within the text.

★ ★ INDEX ★ ★

★ ★ INDEX ★ ★

★ ★ INDEX ★ ★

H

★ ★ INDEX ★ ★

M

★ ★ INDEX ★ ★

O

P

Q

ABOUT THE AUTHOR

Curt Smith is an author, teacher, radio and television commentator and documentarian, and a former presidential speechwriter. *Windows on the White House* is his sixth book. Prior books include *America's Dizzy Dean*, *Long Time Gone*, *Voices of The Game*, *A Fine Sense of the Ridiculous*, and *The Storytellers*.

Smith does essays for Rochester, New York's National Public Radio and NBC-Television affiliates WXXI and WHEC, respectively. He also hosts a series on the Empire Sports TV network, writes for *Reader's Digest,* and teaches Communication at his alma mater, SUNY at Geneseo, and the University of Rochester. Recent documentaries include three 90-minute prime-time ESPN-TV "Voices of The Game" specials Smith wrote and co-produced based upon his book.

Formerly a Gannett reporter, *The Saturday Evening Post* senior editor, and chief speechwriter for President Ronald Reagan's cabinet, Smith wrote more 1989-93 speeches than anyone else for President George Bush. Among them were the "Just War" Persian Gulf address; dedication speeches for the Nixon and Reagan libraries; and speech aboard the battleship USS *Missouri* on the 50th anniversary of Pearl Harbor.

After leaving the White House, he hosted a smash series at the Smithsonian Institution, based on *Voices of The Game*, before turning to radio and TV. Smith lives with his wife Sarah in his hometown of Rochester, and jokes that the Stairway to Heaven favors fans of Broadway musicals, "The Andy Griffith Show," and the Boston Red Sox.